CREATING POLITICAL EQUALITY

AMERICAN ELECTIONS AS A PUBLIC GOOD

JAY R. MANDLE

ACADEMICA PRESS
BETHESDA - DUBLIN - PALO ALTO

Library of Congress Cataloguing-in-Publication Data

Mandle, Jay R. Creating political equality : American elections as a public good / Jay Mandle.
p. cm.
Includes bibliographical references and index.
ISBN-13: 978-1-933146-90-4

1. Campaign funds--United States. 2. Elections—United States. 3. Public goods. 4. United States—Economic policy—2009- 5. United States—Social policy—1993— 6. Medical policy—United States. 7. Environmental policy—United States. I. Title.
JK1991.M259 2010
324.7'80973—dc22

2010001640

Academica Press, LLC
Box 60728
Cambridge Station
Palo Alto, CA. 94306

Website: www.academicapress.com

to order: 650-329-0685

Remembering Paul

Table of Contents

List of Tables

Preface

When I first became interested in political campaign finance, I was surprised to learn that this was a subject without a theory. To be sure, journalistic accounts of how political campaigns are paid for are abundant. Almost all discussions of the American political system make note of the fact that efforts to secure elected office are expensive and invariably are paid for by a wealthy minority of the population. But models have not been offered that can provide insight into the consequences for democracy that result from our system of private campaign financing. Similarly, there exist no systematic considerations of how the content of democracy would be influenced if a system of public funding were utilized.

As a result of these omissions we lack a deep understanding of the contemporary possibilities of democracy. In particular, we do not have a theory of how we might achieve a greater degree of equality in our political system than we possess at present. My intention with this book is to begin to fill that analytic void. I do so by maintaining that the electoral system shares many of the characteristics of a public good and that since it does, political campaigns should be paid for with tax revenues. My argument is that a political system funded by everyone will be more just than one in which candidates for office are required to tap a relative handful of private individuals for financing.

But I hope that this book will do more than contribute to an academic dialogue and represent an advance in democratic theory. My purpose in writing it is also to be of assistance to activists who are engaged in the political effort to make the American political system fairer. I do so as a co-founder in 2000 of the campus-based reform organization, Democracy Matters. Largely financed by my adopted son, Adonal Foyle, from his earnings as a player in the National Basketball Association, Democracy Matters has attracted the support of large numbers of college students eager to construct a political system of greater equality and fairness than the one that exists today.

My involvement with Democracy Matters has been both a source of inspiration and a means by which my own perspective on the subject has been clarified. On-going discussions, particularly at the organization's annual student "Summits," have allowed me to try out my ideas and revise them as needed, all the while drawing on the energy and enthusiasm that DM students have in abundance.

Advocates of social justice in the United States lack a unifying vision. Certainly people on the political left in this country do not possess an effective counter-thrust to the conservative mantra that the society benefits to the extent that the role of the government is reduced. As I argue in this work, that claim is demonstrably false with regard to the substantive issues of global climate change, health care reform, and financial sector regulation. But the absence of an alternative formulation to match the conservative appeal to a miniaturized government has handicapped those who would move the country in a progressive direction. My suggestion is that such an alternative might be to call for political equality to be achieved through the public funding of election campaigns. Accomplishing that objective would reduce the power of wealth in politics and enhance citizen influence. With that, the likelihood of the enactment of equitable legislation in areas of critical concern would be much enhanced.

In writing this book, and in addition to the contribution from discussions with Democracy Matters activists, I have benefited from suggestions made by Lou Ferleger and Jon Mandle. Burt Weltman read the chapters as I drafted them and supplied me with detailed comments on each. That I did not always do as he suggested is not a negative commentary on the value I place on his views. Joan D. Mandle, the Executive Director of Democracy Matters, has been even more intimately involved in this project. She provided me with detailed feedback on everything I wrote. But even before writing, I tried out my ideas and discarded or incorporated them in large part in response to her advice.

Finally, a note concerning the book's dedication. Paul Lyons was a lifelong friend and political collaborator. No two people ever started their analyses from such different sensibilities, only to arrive - nearly always - at the same political conclusions. I am certain that if he were still alive his commentary on the manuscript would have been rich and textured. Paul's premature death is an irretrievable loss.

Chapter 1

The Theory of Elections as a Public Good

Elections are the mechanisms by which government officials in a democracy not only ascend to their positions but also are held accountable for their actions. With elections, voters can either choose continuity in their political representation or opt to send new people to office to implement public policy innovations. Elections provide the means by which citizens articulate their policy preferences. An efficient representative system is one in which the sentiments of an enfranchised citizenry are closely reflected in legislative outcomes.

Democracy requires elections, but running for office requires resources. The electoral process is not immune to the economist's rule that there is no free lunch. Efforts by candidates to make their views known have to be paid for. At the most elementary level, posters require paper that has to be bought and paint that has a price. Even if an artist donates his or her labor, the finished placards must be distributed, involving transportation costs. More realistically, in contemporary society the process by which voters become acquainted with the choices they have in electing representatives is fabulously expensive. Television is the medium through which most people learn about public issues and form their opinions. But even a minimal television advertising campaign racks up costs in the many thousands of dollars. Since electoral campaigns are not free, money to pay for them must be mobilized by office-seekers. In order to have a reasonable chance of success, candidates must either themselves have sufficient wealth to finance their efforts, have access to donors who are willing to provide those resources, or be provided with public funds.

If candidates are unable to raise enough money, their election chances are doomed. Without sufficient financing they will not be able to communicate adequately with the electorate, ruining their chances for victory. Very rarely do citizens vote for candidates with whom they are unfamiliar. The economics of the electoral process therefore is an important determinant of the range of views and candidates presented to the electorate. For there to be a democracy in which a wide array of viewpoints is debated, a political financing system that facilitates extensive candidate participation is essential. Thus, the way office-seekers are financed goes a long way in determining the efficiency of the electoral process. The funding system determines the extent to which a wide variety of opinions and potential candidates can be effectively presented to the voters, enabling them to choose those whose views most closely reflect their own.

Despite its obvious importance, however, the economics of the electoral system is a subject that has been neglected by scholars. I know of no systematic or comparative discussion that considers the extent to which alternative systems of electoral funding influence political outcomes. The result is a gaping void in democratic theory. Without a consideration of how the mechanisms of campaign funding influence political results, we cannot possess a full understanding of how democracy can or should function.

Even the theorist most associated with the view that politics is a market-like phenomenon, Joseph A. Schumpeter, failed to fill this vacuum. The role of the electorate in Schumpeter's model of democracy is to choose among candidates, all of whom have been socialized for political leadership. The process of selection, in Schumpeter's model, is done in the market-like system of the electoral process. Thus Schumpeter approvingly quotes a politician's comment: "What businessmen do not understand is that exactly as they are dealing in oil, so

I am doing in votes."[1] As Tom Bottomore puts it, Schumpeter "formulates an economic definition of democracy, conceived as an institutional arrangement like the market, in which various groups and individuals – equivalent to enterprises and entrepreneurs – compete for the votes of electors, the political 'consumers.'"[2]

What Schumpeter called for was the creation of a professional class of politicians upon whom responsibility for policies would rest. Socialized as an exclusive "social stratum" and thereby endowed "with a professional code and a common fund of views," they could be relied upon not to stray far beyond a cautious political orthodoxy. Policy formation in this way would be left to the office-holding politicians and not emanate from the voters themselves. Schumpeter writes: "the deciding of issues by the electorate [is] secondary to the election of the men who are to do the deciding."[3] His idea of democracy then was designed to use the market for votes as a way, in John Dunn's words, to place "massively effective barriers between the feckless decisions of individual citizens and the consequential choices of those whom they select to rule."[4]

Schumpeter's market analogy, however, is at best incomplete. Though voters do provide votes, they do not provide revenue. In economic theory, the composition of output – the products that firms supply - is ultimately decided by consumers because they pay for the products they purchase. Their choices and the money they spend in support of those choices determine what is profitable for firms to produce and bring to the market. Consumers and their consumption decisions dictate output. But in politics, while office-seekers do compete for votes and the electorate chooses among candidates, those voters do not pay bills. People at the polls do not provide the funds that allow candidates to mount political races. Because voters – even if thought of as consumers in a political marketplace

---

[1] Joseph A. Schumpeter, *Capitalism, Socialism and Democracy*, (First edition, 1942; New York, HarperPerennial, 1976) p. 285.

[2] Tom Bottomore, "Introduction," Joseph A. Schumpeter, *Capitalism, Socialism and Democracy*, p. xi.

[3] Joseph A. Schumpter, *Capitalism, Socialism and Democracy*, p. 261, 290, 269.

[4] John Dunn, "Conclusion," in John Dunn (ed.) *Democracy: The Unfinished Journey, 508 BC to AD 1993* (Oxford: Oxford University Press, 1992), p. 260.

– do not provide resources to office-seekers, they only partially determine who prevails politically.

To be sure, no candidate can ignore the preferences of the voters. The electorate does determine who wins elections. But that power is shared with donors – the people who provide the cash with which candidates mount their campaigns. Voters are not given the choice of voting for a candidate who cannot raise adequate campaign funds, and providing such funds is not the function of the electorate. Just as politicians cannot be indifferent to the wishes of the people who vote, so it is also the case that they cannot ignore the views of the people who pay for their campaigns. The latter in fact determine the extent to which they are able to campaign. It is true that no funder, however deep his or her pockets, can induce a politician to adopt a position that will result in certain electoral defeat. But it is also the case that no political aspirant can fail to take into account the preferences of political contributors.

Because Schumpeter neglects the funding issue, his model also ignores the implications of the fact that the political process shares the characteristics of "public goods." As in economic theory's definition of the latter, the political process produces a socially-needed service that affects more people than actually pay for it. A form of "free-riding" therefore prevails. Only voluntary donors provide the resources to pay for political campaigns.

Free-riding occurs when producers are unable to confine the use of their output to the people who actually pay them, and where consumers are unable to prevent non-payers from sharing their purchases. Economic theory teaches that when these circumstances prevail, markets are undersupplied. Free-riding reduces the profitability of production and therefore product availability.

But cast in a different perspective, the fact that some individuals are willing to pay for an output that is shared with non-payers can be seen as endowing market power to those who avoid the temptation to free-ride. Because such individuals are willing to compensate the producers, they are able to exercise influence over the nature and quality of the product in question. It is one thing to say that the market for shared products is undersupplied. But to the extent that such products nevertheless are made available, power can be exercised by the willing compensators. Particularly when sharing is wide-spread, producers will be sensitive to the preferences of those who pay. The latter are the former's only source of income.

In both economics textbooks and the world of policy-making, this imbalance in influence is avoided by having public goods – products or services whose characteristics mean that by necessity they are shared - paid for by the government. Examples are the providing of roads and highways, police services and national security. The assumption is that in cases like these, free-riding is unavoidable and that furthermore those willing should not be permitted to exercise disproportionate influence over their availability. This is the rationale, as a case in point, for the way the government's defense budget is paid for.

Consider what would happen if defense were paid for privately. Who would foot the bill? Two sources of funds would be possible. One would be from those individuals who choose to contribute to the defense budget for philanthropic and/or patriotic reasons. While not ruling out the possibility that a great number of citizens might well decide to voluntarily contribute, it is unlikely that sufficient funds could be raised from this source alone to adequately defend the country. This insufficiency would emerge because if defense were to depend upon voluntary contributions, many people would be tempted not to pay. Instead they would count on others to provide the funds while they receive the benefits: in short to free ride.

In the face of a resulting shortfall, those in charge of the country's defense would have to appeal to a second potential pool of donors in addition to those who voluntarily contribute for patriotic reasons. These would be potential contributors who, in making a defense donation and supporting the nation's security, would seek to advance their own private interests as well. Successful fundraising among this group would largely be determined by the extent to which national security administrators could creditably promise to cater to the funders.

But in servicing the interests of this second group of donors, defense outlays would in all likelihood become inefficient. Instead of expenditures being measured exclusively by the criterion of achieving national security, that goal would be counter-balanced, at least to some extent, by parochial concerns. Defense fundraisers would have to respond to the preferences of potential funders, whether or not those preferences represented an effective way to achieve national security. Equipment might be purchased based on supplier interests rather than military necessity, or military bases located according to donor preferences rather than sound strategic considerations. The scope for waste and abuse would be extensive.

The remarkable fact is that though it is widely recognized that the provision of public goods such as defense or road construction should not be privately financed, that same recognition is not extended to the most obviously shared process, politics. This omission exists despite the fact that the same mechanism that would produce inefficiencies and distortions with regard to the defense budget exists when elections are paid for privately.

Politics shares the characteristics of public goods since elected officials legislate for everyone – for non-donors and supporters of defeated candidates as well as for the people who vote for and finance the victors. A person who possesses no electoral or financial responsibility for a program or law is no less bound by a political outcome than is someone who votes for a victorious candidate or who helped pay for that victory. But since electoral campaigns are not provided with public funds, those who make financial contributions are able to exercise disproportionate influence over the content of policies that affect the entire citizenry. Politicians are more responsive to those who provide financing than to those who do not.

Such a relationship of reciprocity between donor and candidate does not imply illegality. Its presence simply means that people do not give away their money for no reason and that the recipients will feel at least some degree of obligation to those who underwrite their career successes. In making political contributions, funders increase the likelihood that an objective they seek will be accomplished. Donors are buying an enhanced probability of a candidate's providing them with a desired service.

The problem with this method of funding lies in the fact that with it the preferences of the electorate as a whole are not given the same weight in political decision-making as those who make political contributions. The conflict between private and public interests can be quite stark. Private donors might, for example, expect that in exchange for their funds the office-seeker will adjust his or her legislative votes to satisfy them. Alternatively, and probably more frequently, donors may simply purchase enhanced access to the candidate and with that the opportunity to develop an informal and perhaps influential relationship. A third possibility is that the donor may see in the candidate an incumbent or a potential elected official with whom there is already a shared agreement on policy. In this case, the contribution is made to increase the probability of that candidate's success, a success that would advance the donor's legislative preferences. Whatever its specific form, a reciprocal relationship is involved. The office-seeker needs what the donor can provide - funds. In return, the political contributor attempts to enhance the likelihood that his or her views will be expressed as public policy. In this mutually advantageous relationship, the wider set of interests present in the society is relegated to a status subordinate to the concerns of campaign donors.

Private contributors then are the political counterparts to investors that firms depend on to finance their production and growth. Like those investors, donors make resources available to candidates who need money to compete effectively. In providing such funds, contributors are using their wealth to underwrite a risky project in the hope that they will reap an adequate reward. A campaign contribution is a bet made by an individual that the recipient will not only mount an effective campaign and be elected to office, but also will help to supply the legislative outcomes that are supportive of the donor's interests. What differentiates these activities from normal market behavior is that legislative outcomes are not confined to the donors, but affect the lives of every citizen.[5]

Table 1.1

Mean Campaign Expenditures in 1982-84 prices, 1974-2006

Year	House of Representatives	Senate
1974	108,284	887,387
1978	167,853	1,459,210
1982	236,332	1,846,440
1986	269,710	2,497,991
1990	246,103	1,979,813
1994	296,819	2,694,074
1998	338,935	2,316,273
2002	410,066	2,524,071
2006	493,883	3,929,621

Source: Norman J. Ornstein, Thomas E. Mann and Michael J. Malbin, *Vital Statistics on Congress 2008*, (Washington D.C: Brookings Institution Press, 2008) Tables 3-2 and 3-5. Current dollar expenditures deflated using "Purchasing Power of the Dollar: 1950-2007," U.S. Census Bureau, *Statistical Abstract of the United States: 2009* (Washington D.C. 2008) Table 702.

The importance of how campaigns are funded becomes more significant as they become increasingly expensive. As indicated in Table 1.1, electoral costs in races for a 2006 seat in Congress were, after adjusting for inflation, more than four times higher than they had been in 1974. In and of itself this large increase would not necessarily be alarming. If these sums were raised from a widening

[5] Stephen Ansolabehere, John M. deFigueiredo and James M. Snyder Jr. see political contributions as acts of consumption rather than, as here, investment. See their "Why is There So Little Money in U.S. Politics," *The Journal of Economic Perspectives*, Vol. 17, no. 1 (Winter, 2003) pp. 105-130.

contributor base, the increased cost of running for office might in fact represent a diversification of the donor pool and a democratization of the political process. But if the donor pool remained roughly the same, then the increase in campaign expenditures would represent the reverse. In that case, increased contributions from a still-limited number of donors would enhance the political leverage of those private benefactors. And that in fact is what happened.

No one data source provides complete information concerning the nature of the donor population. The American National Studies Guide to Public Opinion and Electoral Behavior supplies a continuous time series on the percentage of the population that reported making donations to candidates or parties. In addition, The Center for Responsive Politics (CRP) works with reports provided by candidates to the Federal Election Commission (FEC) to estimate the population of contributors. But since the FEC requires that only donations in excess of $200 be itemized, this source omits donors who contributed less than that amount. Further, the CRP data extends back only to 1990. Finally, only a limited amount of survey data are available that supply information concerning the wealth and political attitudes of donors.

Regardless of the source however, no one doubts that the percentage of the American population that makes political contributions is quite low: in a typical year less than 10 percent. Even more dramatically, the percentage that makes contributions of at least $200 is miniscule, always less than 1 percent (Table 1.2).

We will see in Chapter 3 that this small sub-set provided between 80 and 90 percent of the funds received by candidates for the House of Representatives and the Senate in the elections held from 2000 to 2006. As of this writing, survey data on this subject are not yet available for 2008. But in light of Barack Obama's emphasis on small donors during his presidential campaign, it is probable that both the percentage of the population that provided political contributions and the proportion of the population that donated small amounts of money were higher in the 2008 electoral cycle than in the past. Even so, it remains the case that providing political donations involves only a small proportion of the electorate.

Table 1.2

Percent of Population Contributing to a Political Campaign and Percentage of Adult Population Contributing $200 or More to a Political Campaign, 1974-2006

Year	Percent Contributing	Percent Contributing $200 or More
1974	8	NA
1978	13	NA
1982	9	NA
1986	10	NA
1990	7	0.15
1994	6	0.22
1998	7	0.24
2002	11	0.30
2006	NA	0.36

Source: Percent Adult Population that Gave Money: The ANES Guide to Public Opinion and Electoral Behavior,
http://www.electionstudies.org/nesguide/totable/tab6b _5.htm;
Center for Responsive Politics, "Donor Demographics,"
http://www.opensecrets.org.

We will see in Chapter 3 that this small sub-set provided between 80 and 90 percent of the funds received by candidates for the House of Representatives and the Senate in the elections held from 2000 to 2006. As of this writing, survey data on this subject are not yet available for 2008. But in light of Barack Obama's emphasis on small donors during his presidential campaign, it is probable that both the percentage of the population that provided political contributions and the proportion of the population that donated small amounts of money were higher in the 2008 electoral cycle than in the past. Even so, it remains the case that providing political donations involves only a small proportion of the electorate.

The problem is that the small slice of the population that makes substantial political contributions is far from a representative sample of the American people.

Table 1.3

Demographic Characteristics of Political Donors and All Citizens

	Donors	All Citizens
Education		
Graduate Degree	49	10
High School or Less	5	44
Income		
$50,000 or Less	4	65
Above $100,000	78	8
Occupation		
Business Executive and Professionals	92	15
Not Professional Executive and Professionals	6	85

Source: Peter L. Francia, John C. Green, Paul S. Herrnson, Lynda W. Powell, and Clyce Wilcox, *The Financiers of Congressional Elections: Investors, Ideologues and Intimates* (New York: Columbia University Press, 2003), Table 2.4, p. 28.

Table 1.3 provides the data from a 1996 survey of Congressional donors. The results are clear. "Significant donors" – donors who contributed at least $200 to a candidate or party - are richer, better educated, and employed in more prestigious occupations than the population as a whole. In each case the gap is large.

While 44 percent of the population was educated to the level of a high school degree or less, almost half of the campaign donors possessed graduate or professional degrees. Paralleling this, while almost all donors were either business people or professionals, only 15 percent of the population worked in those occupational categories. Not surprisingly therefore, the income gap between donors and the population as a whole is wide. Just about two-thirds of the population earned $50,000 or less while only 4 percent of donors fit that category. More than three-quarters of donors earned $100,000 or more. It is no understatement to conclude, as Francia et al do, that donors constitute "an elite population." They write: "If the donor pool looked like America, one might not care that a small number of donors provide so much of the funding...." But in fact, as they put it, "the donor pool clearly looks like an 'upper class choir.'"[6] The population of political contributors does not resemble anything like a cross-section of the American electorate. The political process is funded by an elite that thereby gains the power to shape political outcomes to its own advantage.

This view of elite donor domination in policy formation is reinforced by Larry M. Bartels' recent research on representation in the American political system. Using Senatorial roll call data and public opinion surveys, Bartels sets for himself the task of first identifying whether United States Senators were more responsive to the views of their wealthy compared to their non-wealthy constituents, and secondly, why this was the case. With regard to the first, the findings are stark. Bartels writes that his statistical results imply that Senatorial roll call votes "were quite responsive to the ideological views of their middle- and high-income constituents. In contrast, the view of low-income constituents had **no** discernible impact on the voting behavior of their senators." When Bartels attempted to find the source of this representational disparity he discovered little or no explanatory power among the variables that political scientists

---

[6] Peter L. Francia, John C. Green, Paul S. Herrnson, Lynda W. Powell, and Clyde Wilcox, *The Financiers of Congressional Elections: Investors, Ideologues and Intimates* (New York: Columbia University Press, 2003) p. 29, 27.

conventionally employ when discussing this subject. He writes that his "results provide surprisingly strong and consistent evidence that the biases I have identified in Senators' responsiveness to rich and poor constituents are **not** primarily due to differences between rich and poor constituents in turnout, political knowledge or contacting."[7]

Bartels does not formally test the hypothesis that this disparity in representation is the consequence of the fact that wealthy people make most of the political contributions while middle and low income people make relatively few. He does provide some limited evidence that this is the case, but the thrust of his discussion is to emphasize the importance of political contributions because other explanations fail. He does not believe that the differences in influence result from the wealthy having higher voting turn-out rates, or because they are better informed about issues than the poor. Differences in the frequency with which affluent and non-affluent people contact office holders do exist, though as Bartels writes, it "is far from the whole story." Rather, "the even simpler assumption that the rich are more influential than the poor because they provide the contributions that fuel contemporary campaigning and lobbying activities receives somewhat stronger support," though he concedes that that support is "quite indirect."[8]

Both theory and evidence then suggest that because the electoral process shares the characteristics of a public good, the fact that it is paid for privately empowers donors to exercise disproportionate influence over the content of political outcomes. The conclusion that follows is that if a democracy requires an accurate representation of citizens' preferences, elections should be treated in the same way as the defense budget. To be fair – that is to be efficient - public funds should be used to pay the expenses involved when candidates run for office.

If the electoral process were financed as a public good, with taxes being used to pay for electoral campaigns, the funding elite's privileged opportunity to

---

[7] Larry M. Bartels, *Unequal Democracy: The Political Economy of the New Gilded Age* (Princeton and Oxford: Princeton University Press, 2008) p. 257, 260. Emphasis in original.
[8] Ibid., p. 279-80.

invest in and thereby shape United States politics would be lost. Politicians would no longer owe their incumbency to donors as well as to the electorate. Elected officials and challengers would not have to consider the risk to their funding that would occur if they endorsed the positions of middle and low income voters. Those voters, who at the moment are underrepresented because they do not make financial contributions, would find a voice and a level of influence not present in our privately funded political system.

There are critics who argue that such a system of public financing of campaigns would violate the First Amendment's prohibition of restrictions on speech. The argument is that because these funds come from tax revenues, taxpayers who oppose publicly funded candidates are denied their First Amendment right not to support an office-seeker. As Chip Mellor writes, "First Amendment freedoms are infringed upon when individuals are compelled to make contributions for political purposes."[9]

But in fact the Supreme Court has ruled on this issue, finding that the provision in the Federal Election Campaign Act (FECA) that created the presidential public funding system did not violate free speech rights. According to the Court, this section of FECA represented a legitimate effort by Congress "to reduce the deleterious influence of large contributions on our political process, to facilitate communications by candidates with the electorate and to free candidates from the rigors of fundraising."[10]

However the Court did not provide a thorough enough discussion of its reasoning. Instead of carefully assessing the rights of taxpayers, the Court confined itself to the cryptic comment that "every appropriation made by Congress uses public money in a manner to which some taxpayers object."[11]

---

[9] Chip Mellor, "Three Lessons from Arizona," in John Samples (ed.) *Welfare for Politicians: Taxpayer Financing of Campaigns* (Washington DC: Cato Institute, 2005) p. 33.

[10] Electronic Privacy Information Center, "Buckley et al v. Valeo, Secretary of the United States et al," 424 U.S. 1, Supreme Court of the United States, Appeal from the United States Court of Appeals for the District of Columbia Circuit, http://www.epic.org/free_speech/buckley_v_valeo.html.

[11] Ibid.

While true, this remark is not sufficient to meet the argument that public financing of elections represents an involuntary, and at least some of the time, a perverse expression of political voice.

What the Court could have done, but did not do, was to place its finding in the context of public goods theory. If it had done so, it would have found ample grounds for defending robust public funding systems for elections. Particularly in a system in which public funding is offered as an option but not a requirement, its effect is to widen the realm of political participation and debate. Rather than denying free speech rights, public funding of campaigns expands speech.

The public funding of elections would enhance political equality without endangering free speech. Such a financing system would serve the country well. For at present our political system is responsive to a small sub-section of the population and thus, as we will see later in this study, produces socially dysfunctional outcomes. As Francia et al put it, "when members of Congress hear more frequently the voice of donors, it creates representational distortion..." contributing "...to the narrow range of policy options that are on the congressional agenda."[12]

---

[12] Ibid., p. 162.

Chapter 2

The History of Campaign Financing

According to Robert E. Mutch, a leading historian of campaign financing in the United States, "a problem that we still are trying to solve: Who should pay for our politics" was first brought to the public's attention in 1839 by a Congressional investigation into campaign fundraising at the U.S. Customhouse in New York.[1] Before that date, "questions about the source of campaign funds and their potential for influencing the successful candidate's behavior in office seldom arose."[2] Still in place at that time was "the deferential political system of the colonial era" in which politics was, as Mutch puts it, "the almost exclusive province of the old mercantile and landed elites." He goes on, "the upper classes provided the bulk of the candidates and they paid for their own campaign expenses."[3] Politics in pre-Jacksonian America "was a gentleman's pursuit."[4]

The transition to a more egalitarian system – one in which people other than those in the top strata of society could run for office with a realistic chance of victory - required the development of new ways of political financing. The problem was, according to Mutch, that "there was precious little in the way of

---

[1] Robert E. Mutch, "The First Federal Campaign Finance Bills," in Paul Baker (ed.), *Money and Politics* (University Park, PA, (The Pennsylvania State University Press, 2002) p. 30.
[2] Robert E. Mutch, *Campaigns, Congress and Courts: The Making of Federal Campaign Finance Law* (New York: Praeger, 1988), p. xvii.
[3] Robert E. Mutch, "The First Federal Campaign Finance Bill," p. 30.
[4] Robert E. Mutch, *Campaigns, Congress and Courts*, p. xv.

political theory and historical example to help legislators make sense of this new problem."[5]

An alternative to personal wealth as the source of political financing appeared with the growth of the spoils and assessment system. The new approach became important for the first time during the presidency of Andrew Jackson (1829 – 1837). Until then what passed for a civil service was staffed by members of the social elite. Michael Nelson notes that forty percent of John Adams' high level appointees were relatives of other high level appointees, and a similar situation prevailed in Jefferson's administration as well. Nelson writes that "kinship as well as class helped to assure the elite character of the early civil service" and that "some subsecretarial American civil servants, like their British counterparts, asserted not only a property right to their offices, but a right of inheritance as well."[6]

It was against these assertions of privilege that Andrew Jackson rebelled, complaining in his first annual message to Congress about an administrative system in which "office is considered a species of property and government…a means of promoting individual interests." Denying the validity of such particularistic objectives, Jackson opined that "the duties of all public officers are, or at least admit of being made, so plain and simple that men of intelligence may readily qualify themselves for their performance."[7] According to Jackson, expertise in the public service was not required.

With this the case, there could be no real objection to elected officials employing untrained party loyalists in government positions. In exchange for their jobs, those employees as a matter of course were expected to contribute a percentage of their salaries to their benefactor's party.[8] Failure to provide such a

---

[5] Robert E. Mutch, "The First Federal Campaign Finance Bills," p. 45.

[6] Michael Nelson, "A Short, Ironic History of American National Bureaucracy," *The Journal of Politics*, Vol. 44, no. 3 (August 1982), p. 758.

[7] As quoted in ibid., p. 759.

[8] Anthony Corrado, "Money and Politics: A History of Federal Campaign Finance Law," in Anthony Corrado, Daniel R. Ortiz, Thomas E. Mann and Trevor Potter (eds.) *The New Campaign Finance Sourcebook* (Washington DC: The Brookings Institution, 2005) p. 8.

"voluntary" contribution was reason for dismissal. As Mark Summers writes "no salary was too modest to be overlooked, from municipal scrubwomen to disabled inmates of soldiers' homes and jailhouse wardens."[9]

Though an absence of data makes it impossible to quantify this pattern, it seems likely that such assessments were the dominant means of political party funding. A pioneer in campaign finance studies, Louise Overacker, writes that throughout the middle of the nineteenth century "at the heart of party finance was the principle of assessment on officeholders in particular and partisans in general,"[10] and Mutch concurs, noting that this system of informal taxation was probably the largest source of campaign funds for both political parties in the nineteenth century.[11]

On one hand the spoils and assessment system meant that for the first time non-elite men were able to hold elected office. An alternative to social connections had become available. Hoogenboom captures what was going on well when he writes, "the spoils system, though hoary in some aspects, [grew] with democracy; it was no accident that the two developed side by side."[12]

On the other hand, as the country modernized and the size of the government bureaucracy did so as well, the inefficiencies associated with the spoils system increased. Contrary to Jackson's view, skills and professional training were important if government services were to be efficiently provided. With party loyalty and financial contributions dominating hiring decisions however, competence was often only marginally present. Furthermore, the ebb and flow of electoral politics tended to undermine efficiency. Whenever a party in

---

[9] Mark Wahlgren Summers, "'To Make the Wheels Revolve We Must Have Grease' Pork Barrel Politics in the Gilded Age," in Paula Baker (ed.) *Money and Politics*, (University Park PA" The Pennsylvania State University Press, 2002) p. 60.

[10] Louise Overacker, *Money in Elections* (Reprint Edition New York: Arno Press, 1974; first published by The Macmillan Company, 1932), p. 126.

[11] Robert E. Mutch, "The First Federal Campaign Finance Bills," p. 30, 45.

[12] Ari Hoogenboom, *Outlawing the Spoils: A History of the Civil Service Reform Movement, 1865-1883*, (Urbana: University of Illinois Press, 1961) p. 4.

opposition was successful and ascended to office, new appointees replaced former employees, causing organizational disruption.

Over time concerns with these inefficiencies triggered political efforts to professionalize the civil service.[13] The Pendleton Act of 1883 was the legislative means by which this was achieved. That act classified some government positions as outside the reach of political hiring and firing. Thereafter, a growing number of government-protected positions were created and filled using meritocratic criteria in a system administered by the newly established Civil Service Commission.

Electoral campaigns however had never been entirely dependent upon assessments. Self-funded candidates still ran for office and voluntary private contributions were made as well, even during the mid-nineteenth century - the hey-day of the spoils system.[14] Overacker puts it this way: "the money which cannot be extracted from candidates or office-holders must be obtained from 'the public' generally. This is a very broad classification which includes groups as varied as the organized criminal element of our large cities, corporations and individuals who seek special favors and those voters whose gifts are prompted by an interest in the success of the party's program, rather than the hope of any immediate personal return."[15] Summers reports "in every campaign, party leaders plotted to open up wallets up and down Wall Street."[16]

As the financial yield coming from political appointees declined because of the Pendleton Act, the spoils and assessment system became an inadequate source of political party funding. As the share of the federal bureaucracy shielded by the Civil Service Commission grew, freed from the dunning of a previous era, Overacker's "public" became, of necessity, an increasingly important source of political funds. Corrado summarizes the transition that occurred: "the [Pendelton] act reduced the reliance of party organization on government employee contributions and shifted the burden of party fundraising to corporate interests,

---

[13] Ari Hoogenboom, *Outlawing the Spoils*, p. 8.
[14] Robert E. Mutch, "The First Federal Campaign Finance Bills," p. 39.
[15] Louise Overacker, *Politics and People*, p. 105.
[16] Mark Wahlgren Summers, "'To Make the Wheels Revolve We Must have Grease,'" p. 57.

especially the industrial giants in oil, railroads, steel and finance, which held major stakes in the direction of government policy." Corrado concludes that "business leaders and the corporations they headed were a source of campaign funding before the 1880s but after the adoption of the civil service reforms they became the principal source."[17]

The unforeseen consequence of the Pendleton Act then was to shift political fundraising from a hybrid approach in which money from assessments and donations by private and corporate contributors were both of importance. In its place emerged a financing system that was much more narrowly based. Hoogenboom reports that "...when the elimination of assessments deprived political bosses of a prime source of revenue, businessmen supplied money and dictated policy...The merit system provided the man of business with a more efficient civil service and at the same time increased his power."[18]

It did not take long for that power to be questioned. According to the historian Lewis L. Gould, during the Progressive Era – the mid-1890s to end of World War I - "citizens' groups, angry at poor public facilities, tax favoritism and corruption, waged local campaigns against business privileges and excesses...." Journalists and Congressional committees revealed "the impact of corporate lobbying and campaign donations on lawmakers and government officials." As Gould puts it, "the 'money trust,' Wall Street, or 'Invisible Government' were, for many reform-minded Americans, the dangerous offspring of an unrestrained business community."[19]

Despite the fact that progressives wished to bring big businesses under the control and regulation of government, campaign finance reform was not a priority issue for them. None of the principal historians of the progressive era such as Richard Hofstader or Michael McGerr even raise the issue in their studies of the

---

[17] Anthony Corrado, "Money and Politics: A History of Federal Campaign Finance, Law," p. 10.

[18] Ari Hoogenboom, "The Pendleton Act and the Civil Service," *The American Historical Review*, Vol. 64, no. 2 (January 1959), p. 317.

[19] Lewis L. Gould, "The Progressive Era," in Lewis L. Gould (ed.) *The Progressive Era* (Syracuse: Syracuse University Press, 1974), p. 1, 2-3.

period.[20] Nevertheless it is true that during these years a spate of campaign finance laws was passed. Though campaign financing did not occupy an explicit place on their agenda, progressives were forced to face the issue when scandals emerged involving the financing of parties and candidates. The irony here is that the most important scandal in this regard involved Theodore Roosevelt, the archetype of progressivism in this period.

In 1904 the Democratic candidate for President, Alton B. Parker, charged that his opponent, Roosevelt, had been funded by corporations that had been granted immunity from antitrust law suits. Roosevelt denied the charge, though a subsequent Senate investigation revealed that corporations had indeed provided most of the money for Roosevelt's 1904 campaign, with only four large firms responsible for one-fourth of all his donations. Roosevelt's response to the resulting political uproar was to try to defuse the issue by becoming a champion of reform, calling in 1905 for the public disclosure of campaign funding, a call he repeated in 1906. Roosevelt went even further in 1907 when he advocated a ban on corporate political contributions. That this was more a political ploy than a serious commitment to reform is suggested by the fact that Roosevelt's efforts on behalf of these reforms were tepid at best. Corrado notes that Roosevelt "did not follow up his use of the bully pulpit with a specific legislative proposal or a lobbying effort to force Congress to act."[21]

Nevertheless the Tillman Act banning political contributions by nationally chartered banks and corporations was passed in 1907. An early version had been introduced in 1901 by a Republican Senator from New Hampshire, William E. Chandler. Ignored at the time, it gained traction during the hearings of a New York State legislative committee into the political power of insurance companies in that state. In the course of investigating this subject, Charles Evens Hughes, the

---

[20] Richard Hofstadter, *The Age of Reform: From Bryan to F.D.R.* (New York Vintage Books, 1955); Michael McGerr, *A Fierce Discontent: The Rise and Fall of the Progressive Movement in America, 1870-1920* (New York: Free Press, 2003).

[21] Robert E. Mutch, *Campaigns, Congress and the Courts*, pp. 1-2, 10; Anthony Corrado, "Money and Politics," p. 17.

chief counsel of the committee, discovered that one of the insurance companies had donated almost $50,000 to the Republican National Committee and that it had also done so earlier, in both 1896 and 1900. It was only then that Roosevelt became a supporter of Chandler's bill, though by this time Chandler himself no longer was a member of Congress and it received no support at all from House Republicans. Later, the bill was introduced by the Populist Democrat Benjamin R. "Pitchfork Ben" Tillman. Enough controversy was generated so that in an effort to appease public opinion the Republicans in 1907 supported the bill that was passed and signed by the President.[22]

During the debates on the Tillman Act in 1907 there was also discussion about requiring parties to disclose the sources of their income. Pressure for the enactment of such legislation was mounted by an organization composed of a number of prominent citizens, the National Publicity Law Organization (NPLO). These individuals saw disclosure as a way of protecting corporate shareholder interests. The leader of the NPLO thought that once political committees had to publicly disclose the size and sources of campaign contributions, shareholders would have the information necessary to bring suit against corporate managers. The Federal Corrupt Practices Act ("The Publicity Bill"), passed in 1910, included the language of disclosure though it was weakened in debate and rendered largely ineffective.[23] A year later, in 1911, the Publicity Bill was amended to establish spending limits for federal campaigns. This act too was inadequately enforced and in 1925 ruled to be unconstitutional by the Supreme Court. Then in 1925, in response to the Teapot Dome scandal involving political donations by Harry F. Sinclair during the 1920 election in exchange for the leasing of government oil land to his Sinclair Oil Corporation, another Federal Corrupt Practices Act was passed further extending, in principle, the reach of the law.

---

[22] Robert E. Mutch, *Campaigns, Congress and Courts*, p. 2, 7.
[23] Anthony Corrado, "Money and Politics," p. 13.

Despite this flurry of activity, Sorauf writes that "the regulatory reality was defined by enforcement, not by the words of the statue books. And the reality was one of pervasive evasion and nonenforcement."[24] Corrado agrees, concluding that "an effective regulatory regime was never established" with regard to campaign funding.[25] Though the law was clear concerning reporting requirements, it did not specify who would have access to the reports, did not require that they be published, and did not stipulate penalties for failing to adhere to the law. Similarly, the legislatively-imposed spending limits were widely ignored since the provisions of the law made it easy to circumvent its intention. Writing in 1932, Overacker notes that "as there is not a single instance of the prosecution of a party official for failure to comply with the provisions of the [1925 Corrupt Practices] law, it seems fair to say that these criminal provisions have been of little effect except as a deterrent."[26] With all of this the case, Julian E. Zelizer accurately summarizes the situation, writing that "the Progressive Era had a negligible effect. Candidates easily found loopholes to evade unenforced regulations."[27]

Insight into how the post-Pendleton system worked in practice is provided by data Overacker pieced together from Congressional hearings on the funding of the four presidential elections between 1916 and 1928 (See Table 2.1). Using Overacker's information, I calculated the amount of money the national parties secured in very large contributions of $1,000 or more. That a political donation of $1,000 was a contribution that only could be made by the rich is suggested by the fact that that sum was considerably larger than the $705 which represented the

---

[24] Frank J. Sorauf, *Money in American Elections* (Glenview: Scott, Foresman and Company, 1988), p. 32.
[25] Anthony Corrado, "Money and Politics," p. 15.
[26] Louise Overacker, *Money in Elections*, (New York: Arno Press, 1974; First published by The Macmillan Company, 1932), p. 254.
[27] Julian E. Zelizer, "Seeds of Cynicism: The Struggle over Campaign Finance, 1956-1974," in Paula Baker (ed.) *Money and Politics*, p. 76.

Table 2.1

Number of Contributors of $1,000 or More to the Democratic and Republican National Committees, 1916-1928

Democrats

Year	Number of Contributors	Percent of Contributors	Percent of Money Received
1916	187	0.11	45.3
1920	168	NA	41.7
1924	115	NA	60.8
1928	619	0.68	69.7

Republicans

Year	Number of Contributors	Percent of Contributors	Percent of Money Received
1916	451	1.32	62.3
1920	1072	2.11	33.1
1924	1071	1.19	55.0
1928	1367	0.95	68.4

Source: Calculated from Louise Overacker, *Politics and People*, (Reprint Edition, New York: Arno Press, 1974; first published by The Macmillan Company, 1932) Table XXIX, pp. 132-3.

average annual individual earnings in the United States in 1916.[28] Yet in the four presidential elections between 1916 and 1928, donors of $1,000 or more were responsible for at least 40 percent of the funds collected in those election years. In

---

[28] Richard Sutch and Susan B. Carter (eds.) *Historical Statistics of the United States, Earliest Times to the Present* (New York: Cambridge University Press, 2006) Series Ba4280, 2-265.

the 1928 election, few people - less than one percent of donors to either party - were responsible for almost 70 percent of each party's revenue. Thus throughout this period very few people – no more than roughly 2,000 individuals - gave the lion's share of political contributions.

By the 1930s, as Corrado writes, "it was well known that candidates and party committees were not complying with the dictates of federal law."[29] Nevertheless, campaign finance reform was not on the New Deal agenda. Until the passage of the Hatch Act in 1939, no new legislation concerning campaign financing was adopted. And indeed, that legislation and its 1940 amendments are better understood as an attack on the New Deal than as a serious effort to grapple with the problem of how to pay for politics. The Hatch Act was the product of the concerns of a coalition of Republicans and Southern Democrats about the potential for left-wing political activism by employees of the Works Progress Administration. The act banned political activity by those workers and made it illegal to solicit political funds from them.[30] Similarly, almost ten years later, the 1947 passage of the Taft-Hartley Act, which among other things banned the use of union treasury funds for political donations, can better be understood as an effort to retreat from the New Deal's support for organized labor than as an attempt to seriously reform the way politics was paid for.

But even these campaign finance laws, like those before them, largely were ineffective. George Thayer argues that the Hatch Act was violated repeatedly since "career bureaucrats, if they bothered at all to be subtle, contributed through nominees when they were not being dunned privately at the office by their superiors."[31] Regulations concerning corporate and union campaign donations too were easily evaded. Both groups were able to avoid the intent of the law by donating money to Political Action Committees (PACs)

[29] Anthony Corrado, "Money and Politics," p. 16.
[30] George Thayer, *Who Shakes the Money Tree? American Campaign Financing Practices from 1789 to the Present*, (New York: Simon and Schuster, 1973) p. 71.
[31] Ibid., p. 72.

which then in turn provided candidates with contributions. Thus in practice, private political contributions through the 1950s and 1960s remained unregulated.

Despite or perhaps because of these breakdowns, Alexander Heard in his 1960 book, *The Costs of Democracy*, reported that new ideas were being advocated to correct the failed regulatory approaches of the past. Heard had been a consultant to the Senate's Subcommittee on Privileges and Elections and writes that starting in 1955 reformers had become less interested in efforts to limit expenditures and contributions. Instead, he argued that a new consensus was emerging with three broadly stated goals. They were 1) all candidates with popular support "should be able to compete on reasonably equitable financial terms," 2) candidates should be able to obtain that financial backing "without mortgaging their political souls" and 3) the reforms to accomplish these goals "should be accomplished in a way that creates confidence in the electoral system…." Heard himself believed that since political campaigns are essential to American democracy, "it is appropriate to give them every form of government support that is necessary and feasible." He singled out tax deductions or tax credits as mechanisms that would not only enhance the flow of funds to politicians, but in addition would "improve the respectability and ease of fund-raising."[32]

The increased interest in campaign finance reform that Heard discussed was further stimulated in the aftermath of the 1960 election. Following the contest between John F. Kennedy and Richard M. Nixon there was concern that political campaigns were becoming increasingly expensive. The absence of data here makes it hard to be conclusive. Nevertheless with the growing use and cost of television advertising, Heard accepted as a "plausible inference that total campaign costs at all levels had actually risen."[33]

---

[32] Alexander Heard, *The Costs of Democracy: Financing American Political Campaigns* (Garden City: Anchor Books, 1962 (first published, 1960), p. 10, 11.
[33] Ibid., p. 436.

Further, there was a wide-spread belief that Kennedy's victory was in large part due to his use of his family's wealth. In this regard W.J. Rorabaugh cites Hubert Humphrey as lamenting that the 1960 primary elections proved that "no financially poor candidate, unless there were rich backers, would ever again be able to run for president."[34] Thayer estimates that the Kennedy family spent as much as $4 million in support of John F. Kennedy's presidential aspirations. As Thayer puts it, the manner in which campaign funds were raised and spent in 1960 "caused concern among many thoughtful citizens."[35]

Given the data that are available it is not in fact possible to estimate accurately the extent to which the Kennedy fortune was actually responsible for the outcome of the 1960 election. Herbert Alexander compiled a list of about 5,300 individuals who contributed $500 or more to the Democratic and Republican party campaigns during that election cycle. This group, he estimates, gave in the aggregate about $8.5 million, or about 40 percent of what he describes as "political spending at the national level."[36] But the Kennedy family was not among the 12 "prominent families" Alexander lists. This omission occurred because the Kennedys were not included in the Congressional study of the 1956 election, the list upon which Alexander depended.[37]

What Alexander was able to confirm however was the continuing importance of large donors, a pattern that Overacker had first identified in the 1920s. Alexander and Overacker's classifications of big donors are not the same, with the latter using a cut-off of $1,000 and the former $500. It therefore is not possible to identify a long-term trend in their importance. But as reproduced in Table 2.2, Alexander's data make clear that big donations were the principle source of campaigns funds in the four post-war elections through 1960. Only in

---

[34] W.J. Rorabaugh, *The Real Making of the President: Kennedy, Nixon and the 1960 Election* (Lawrence KS: University Press of Kansas (2009), p. 198.
[35] George Thayer, *Who Shakes the Money Tree?*, p. 19-20, 23.
[36] Herbert E. Alexander, *Financing the 1960 Election* (Princeton N.J.: Citizen's Research Foundation, n.d.) p. 59.
[37] Ibid. p. 60-1.

1956 did the Democrats secure less than 50 percent of their funds from large donations. In the other years both parties raised close to or more than 60 percent of their revenue in the form of $500 or more contributions.

Table 2.2

Contributions of $500 or More as a Percent of Funds Collected by Republican and Democratic National Campaign Committees, 1948-1960

	1948	1952	1956	1960
Democratic	69	63	44	59
Republican	74	68	74	58

Source: Herbert E. Alexander, *Financing the 1960 Election* (Princeton: Citizens' Research Foundation, n.d.) p. 57.

Even before his nomination, Kennedy had expressed unease about the burden of political fundraising on candidates, and once in office he called for reform. At a press conference in May 1961, he declared himself in favor of "some system by which the major burdens of presidential campaigns on both sides would be sustained by the national government."[38] He followed up by creating a Presidential Commission on Campaign Costs, asking its nine members to make "recommendations with respect to improved ways of financing expenditures required of nominees for the offices of President and Vice President."[39]

The Chair of the Commission and its Executive Director were the previously mentioned Alexander Heard and Herbert Alexander respectively, scholars who had collaborated in the past and who were in broad agreement with each other concerning both the need for and content of future reform. The tone

---

[38] Alexander Heard, *The Costs of Democracy: Financing American Political Campaigns,* 419, 420.

[39] *Financing Presidential Campaigns: Report of the President's Commission on Campaign Costs, Financing Presidential Campaigns* (April 1962), p. iii.

and the substance of the Commission's final report were heavily influenced by their shared views. Like Heard, Alexander believed both that "political parties that are beholden to a small number of large contributors constitute an unhealthy element in the body politic" and that "it is clearly in the public interest to find means by which political parties and campaigns can be regularly and adequately financed in ways that will be free of public suspicion."[40]

Reflecting these views, the Commission sought to identify how public policy could increase private voluntary political contributions and thereby widen the funding base supporting electoral candidacies. The Commission's report maintained that "no problem...has become more troublesome than that of providing adequate financial support for campaigns." It declared further that it was "unfortunate" that there was a "lurking suspicion that contributing to political parties is somehow a shoddy business." According to the Commission, "while the great majority of such contributors to presidential campaigns is not motivated by expectation of specific preferment, nonetheless for the vitality and acceptance of the democratic system," it sought to achieve "a significant increase in the number of contributors, both to spread the cost of campaigns and to diffuse more widely through the population the sense and the reality of participation in the politics of democracy."[41] To that end its most important recommendations were that political contributors be given a choice of either a 50 percent tax credit up to a maximum of $100 per year, or a tax deduction for the full amount of contributions up to $1,000 per year. It also argued that an effective system of public disclosure should be adopted in which contributions of $250 or more would be itemized.[42]

Notably absent from this list are any recommendations to limit either campaign expenses or donations. This clearly reflects Heard's view. In *The Costs of Democracy* he had written that "past legislation has almost invariably been negative in character, restricting the uses or amounts of expenditures." They had

---

[40] Ibid., p. 379-80, 11; Herbert E. Alexander, *Financing the 1960 Election*, p. 90.
[41] *Financing Presidential Campaigns*, p. 2, 11.
[42] Ibid., p. 4, 5.

led, he argued "to all sorts of impossible demands on the conduct of those whose lot it is to make self-government in the United States succeed."[43]

In the immediate aftermath of the Kennedy assassination the Commission's report was ignored. Nevertheless its ideas soon resurfaced. The stage had been set for the beginning of the most active period of campaign finance reform in United States history.

---

[43] Alexander Heard, *The Costs of Democracy*, p. 9, 10.

Chapter 3

The Power of Big Donors

Candidates for the United States Congress must collect contributions from private individuals in order to contest both primary and general elections. These fundraising efforts are governed by the Federal Election Campaign Act Amendments Act (FECA) of 1974 and the Bipartisan Campaign Reform Act (BCRA) passed and signed into law in 2002. As interpreted by the Supreme Court, Congressional candidates are under no constraints with regard to their expenditures, though limits are imposed on the amount of money that an individual may contribute to a candidate's campaign. FECA also provides presidential aspirants with an alternative to private fundraising. They can volunteer to participate in a public funding system. With this option, in exchange for agreeing to limit their expenditures, candidates in primary elections receive a public grant that matches private donations to their campaigns up to a specified maximum. In the general election they receive an outright grant that sets the limits of their campaign expenditures.

The Center for Responsive Politics (CRP) categorizes contributions made to candidates for Congress in five groupings: contributions from large donations (over $200); contributions from small donors (under $200); contributions from Political Action Committees (PACs); contributions candidates make to themselves (self-financed); and other. In Table 3.1 these categories are collapsed into two groups. In the first, large donors are added to PACs and self-financed candidates. The remaining category contains small donors and the residual category. The intent in organizing the data in this way is to identify the extent of

Table 3.1

Percent of Campaign Contributions Received by Members of Congress by Level and Source of Contribution, 2000-2006

	House Democrats	Senate Democrats	House Republicans	Senate Republicans
2000				
>$200,PACs, Self	80	82	79	70
<$200,Other	20	18	21	30
2002				
>$200,PACs, Self	85	79	84	79
<$200,Other	15	21	16	21
2004				
>$200,PACs, Self	86	77	91	89
<$200,Other	14	23	9	11
2006				
>$200,PACs, Self	86	72	87	81
<$200,Other	14	28	13	19
2008				
>$200, PACs, Self[1]	91	85	84	87
<$200,Other	9	15	16	13

[1] For 2008 Self-financing is not reported separately.

Source: Calculated from Center for Responsive Politics, "Where the Money Came From," http://www.opensecrets.org.

big donor dominance in political investment. Dominance by large donors, business related PACs, and wealthy self-financing politicians can be taken as evidence in support of the hypothesis that large investors shape the content of political discourse.

Grouping the data in this way somewhat overstates big donor dominance. Unions in the United States are heavily involved in providing funds to candidates through the PACs that they establish. Nevertheless, the table does not distort reality. As was true in the past, during the 2007-2008 election cycle the business community dominated PAC contributions. Business-related PACs outspent those supported unions by more than 4 to 1 in the run-up to the 2008 election.[1]

The pattern revealed in Table 3.1 could not be clearer. Irrespective of party, the funding base for members of Congress is extremely narrow, depending heavily on big donors. Typically, at least 80 percent of the funds received by candidates come from private donors contributing more than $200 (including the candidates themselves) and PACs. Indeed, this percentage has increased since the 2000 elections. Members of both parties in the House and the Senate saw an increase in the importance of big contributors over these years. Most prominent in this upward trend was the experience of House Democrats, who in 2008 received 91 percent of their funding in the form of large donations, in contrast to 80 percent in 2000. In short, these data support the view that with regard to members of Congress, political investment is primarily a big donor activity. Only 0.35 percent of the adult population provided political donations of $200 or more during the 2007-2008 electoral cycle, and this money constituted the overwhelming bulk of the funds candidates received.[2]

Though Joseph A. Schumpeter did not identify campaign financing as the mechanism to make certain that legislators possess "a common fund of views," such a relative uniformity of outlook is achieved when political campaigns

---

[1] Calculated from Center for Responsive Politics, "PACs by Industry," http://www.opensecrets.org.

[2] Center for Responsive Politics, "Donor Demographics," http://www.opensecrets.org.

depend on a small group of private benefactors. Only politicians whose views fall within the limits of the political spectrum represented by large contributors will receive the funding necessary for political success. To be sure, there are disagreements among the donors and thus complete homogeneity in viewpoints does not prevail among candidates. It is also true that donor investment decisions do have to take into account perceived voter preferences. The electorate ultimately does provide the votes necessary to win office. Nevertheless, as Schumpeter would have hoped, wealthy individuals – by making large campaign contributions - define the limits of political acceptability.

Congressional incumbents almost always have more money to spend on their campaigns than do their opponents, and they almost always are re-elected if they choose to run (Table 3.2). In 2002 and 2006, House challengers were able to raise only 63.6 and 60.0 percent of the funds received by incumbents respectively. An even more dramatic shortfall occurred in 2004 when that figure was 36.9 percent. In Senate races the disparity was about at the same level. Challengers for Senate seats typically raised only about 40 percent of the funding that went to incumbent Senators. It will not come as a surprise that in the three election cycles since 2002, House incumbents running for re-election have achieved a success rate well in excess of 90 percent. In the Senate the incumbent re-election rate is almost as high.

It is possible to have a legitimate debate about the role played by the disparity in funding in the overwhelming incumbent success rate. It can be argued that the high re-election rate occurs because incumbents are able to raise more money than their opponents. It is possible that very large war chests were decisive even for relatively unpopular political figures. Those funds could at once have discouraged the emergence of strong opponents and also allowed incumbents to flood the airwaves with effective political ads. But it also can be argued that their victories occurred because the voters were satisfied with the jobs they were doing. The superiority of their fundraising might have been the reward offered for doing a good job. But whichever way causality runs, two principles hold. Candidates cannot win unless they raise large amounts of money and therefore large donors occupy a strategically important role in the political process.

Table 3.2

Success Rate of Congressional Incumbents Seeking Reelection and Mean Challenger Campaign Funds as a Percent of Incumbent Campaign Fund, 2002-2006

	House		**Senate**	
	Incumbent Success Rate	Challenger funds as percent of Incumbent	Incumbent Success Rate	Challenger Funds as percent of Incumbent
2002	96.2	63.6	88.9	38.9
2004	92.9	36.9	96.2	31.4
2006	94.0	60.0	78.6	40.4

Source: Calculated from Norman J. Ornstein, Thomas E. Mann and Michael J. Malbin, *Vital Statistics on Congress, 2008* (Washington DC: Brookings Institution Press, 2008), Tables 2-7, 2-8, 3-2, 3-4.

A question that emerges in this context is the extent to which the 2002 passage of BCRA affected this pattern. That act introduced important changes to the private political funding system by prohibiting parties and candidates from raising soft (unregulated) funds. But at the same time it increased the amount of money that individual funders were allowed to contribute to candidates. With BCRA, during an electoral cycle individuals could contribute $4,600 instead of $2,300 (as before) to individual candidates; $25,000 instead of $20,000 to individual party committees; and $10,000 instead of $5,000 to state or local party committees. After BCRA it became permissible for an individual to make political contributions of $95,000 in an election cycle compared to the previous limit of $50,000.[3]

Reflecting on the content of these BCRA provisions, observers were divided concerning the likely consequence of the legislation. Some thought that the soft money prohibition would force parties and candidates to seek out small donors, raising the importance of the latter group. Others however believed that the big increase in allowable contributions to candidates would result in a strengthening of in the importance of large donors to campaigns.

As revealed in Table 3.3, in the 2003/04 election cycle, following the passage of BCRA, contributions of $1,000 or more became more important as a source of funding than in the previous election cycle, and stayed at roughly that new higher level in 2005/06. Irrespective of party or whether the candidate was an incumbent or a challenger, the pattern was the same. In every case, $1,000 or above contributions as a percentage of campaign funds increased once BCRA was implemented. Indeed for both Republican and Democratic incumbents running for re-election, almost half of all the funds collected were in the form of these very large contributions. At the Congressional level there is no ambiguity. Big donors have become ever more important. As Michael J. Malbin and Sean A. Cain report, "the higher ceiling meant that congressional candidates could raise more without scrambling to recruit new small donors into the system."[4]

Though it may not be quite so obvious, big donors too have in recent years come to dominate the financing of presidential campaign efforts. Between 1976 and 1996, every major party candidate for the presidency participated in the FECA-created public matching system for primary elections and the full public funding for general elections. That pattern however was broken in 2000 and in the years thereafter. Though the Democratic candidate in 2000, Al Gore, accepted

---

[3] Jay R. Mandle, *Democracy, America and the Age of Globalization* (New York: Cambridge University Press, 2008), p. 74-5.

[4] Michael J. Malbin and Sean A. Cain, *The Ups and Downs of Small and Large Donors* (Washington DC: The Campaign Finance Institute, 2007 *www.cfinst.org*) p. 5.

Table 3.3

Contributions of $1,000 or More as Percentage of Total Campaign Funds Raised by Party and Incumbent or Challenger Status, 2001/02-2005/06

House of Representatives

	Democrats		Republicans	
	Incumbents	Challengers	Incumbents	Challengers
2001/02	20	16	21	20
2003/04	30	23	30	31
2005/06	28	31	30	31

Senate

	Democrats		Republicans	
	Incumbents	Challengers	Incumbents	Challengers
2002/02	26	27	26	25
2003/04	42	32	43	31
2005/06	47	32	45	29

Source: Michael J. Malbin and Sean A. Cain, *The Ups and Downs of Small and Large Donors* (The Campaign Finance Institute, 2007), *www.cfinst.org*) Tables A7 and A8.

both matching funds and his entitlement for the general election, George W. Bush opted out of the system of public support for the primary race. Bush nevertheless did participate in the publicly-financed system in the November election.

In 2004 however there was a further retreat from the public funding system. George W. Bush, running for re-election, again chose not to participate in the partially-funded nominating process. But this time he was joined in opting out of the matching grant system for the primary by the leading Democratic Party contenders, John Kerry, the ultimate victor in the Democratic Party primaries, and Howard Dean. Both Bush and Kerry, the nominees of the Republican and Democratic Parties respectively, agreed to accept public funds in the general election.

In the most recent electoral cycle, 2007-2008, the presidential public funding system was further damaged. None of the leading candidates, John McCain, Barack Obama, or Hillary Clinton, accepted matching grants for their primary election campaigns. And for the first time since 1976, one of the nominees, Obama, opted out as well from the public funding system for the general election. Obama's decision to rely on private funding allowed him to massively outspend his Republican opponent during the campaign. While McCain was limited to his public grant, Obama was constrained only by the amount of money he could raise. And he turned out to be a prodigious fundraiser. The CRP estimate is that including both the primary and general election Obama raised $745 million, slightly more than twice the $368 million that was generated for McCain.[5]

Especially in light of this disparity, it is all but certain that in the absence of a radical upward adjustment in the amount of public money available for presidential aspirants, the trend toward private financing will continue. Because of the handicap that it now represents, the presidential funding system will likely be avoided by all serious candidates in the future. The support it provides is

[5] Center for Responsive Politics, "Presidential," http://opensecrets.org.

insufficient when compared to the amount of money major candidates can raise by relying on private sources. It is not so much that the system is broken, but rather that it is dramatically underfunded. Publicly funded candidates are placed at too great a handicap. As John C. Green writes, "the simple answer is that the parameters of the system no longer fit the realities of the presidential nomination system." The problem, he goes on, is that "both the resources available and the spending limits imposed make the system increasingly unattractive to the strongest candidates."[6]

Table 3.4

Payouts from the Presidential Election Fund and Presidential Campaign Expenditures, 1976-2004 ($ millions)

Year	Payout	Expenditures	Expenditures as percent of payout
1976	72.6	66.9	92
1980	103.3	92.3	89
1984	133.5	103.6	78
1988	178.2	210.7	118
1992	175.4	192.2	110
1996	236.0	239.9	102
2000	239.5	343.1	143
2004	207.5	717.9	346

Source: Calculated from Kelly D. Patterson, "Spending in the 2004 Election," in David B. Magleby, Anthony Corrado and Kelly D. Patterson (eds.) *Financing the 2004 Election* (Washington DC: The Brookings Institution, 2006), Tables 3-2 and 3-4.

---

[6] John C. Green, "Financing the 2004 Presidential Nomination Campaigns," in David B. Magleby, Anthony Corrado and Kelly D. Patterson (eds.) *Financing the 2004 Election* (Washington DC: Brookings Institution Press, 2006), p. 120.

The counterpart to the weakening of the presidential public funding system is the increase that has occurred in candidates' reliance on private fundraising. Table 3.4 brings together the payouts from the presidential election campaign fund that have been made since 1976 and available estimates of presidential campaign expenditures for these same years. The data show that from 1976 through 1996 public funding paid for just about all presidential expenditures. But as candidates started to opt out of the matching grant system for primaries, that relationship changed. In the 2004 election cycle, expenditures exceeded the public contribution to the campaigns by almost three and a half fold. Private investment in presidential political campaigns had become dominant.

There was nothing very surprising about George W. Bush's 2004 shift to private funding for his primary campaigns. He was, writes John C. Green and Nathan S. Bigelow, "the very definition of a well-connected party insider and he based his fundraising strategy on exploiting his unique connections with the Republican establishment." To that end, he recruited people who collected or "bundled" $100,000 or more in donations, designating his big fundraisers as "Pioneers." Nothing on this scale had ever been tried before and the strategy paid off. Over two hundred people achieved "Pioneer" status, and together they provided about one-fourth of the funds raised on Bush's behalf.[7]

This Republican shift to private investors can be explained as a return to the orthodox historical pattern of relying on elite donations. But Democrats who rejected public funding in the primaries justified their decision on what they claimed to be the more principled basis of creating a small donor funding system. This defense was offered most forcefully by Joe Trippi, an influential figure in Howard Dean's effort to secure the Democrat's presidential nomination. Dean was the first Democrat to reject the matching system for primaries (John Kerry followed suit) and Trippi suggested that his doing so was a way to break the hold

[7] John C. Green and Nathan S. Bigelow, "The 2000 Presidential Nominations: The Costs of Innovation," in David B. Magleby (ed.) *Financing the 2000 Election* (Washington DC: The Brookings Institution, 2002), p. 59.

of wealthy special interests. Trippi argued that large numbers of $100 donations would be sufficient to "take back the White House and the Congress." He described this as the "$100 Revolution," and elsewhere as "Jefferson's Revenge." But in any case, he argued that the internet could be used to mobilize small donors, and that the technology that allowed political campaigns to do so was "the most democratizing innovation we've ever seen – more so than the printing press."[8]

The Dean campaign's success in using computer technology to raise funds and mobilize supporters aroused the interest of reformers. Most importantly, this strategy attracted the attention of Barack Obama. Four years after the Dean innovation, Obama, explaining why he was considering dropping out of the public funding system for the general election, claimed that his campaign had "... created a parallel public financing system where the American people decide if they want to support a campaign, they can get on the internet and finance it. And they will have as much access and influence over the course and direction of our campaign that has traditionally reserved for the wealthy and the powerful (sic)." Shortly after Obama made these remarks, Robert Bauer his campaign attorney reiterated the point. Interviewed on the Diane Rehm Show, Bauer argued that "Senator Obama is already running what you could call an unprecedentedly publicly financed campaign." He went on: "the explosion of small donor contributions through the internet...is really transforming the face of campaign finance." As such, Bauer concluded, "all of the goals of the public financing system that have generally been heralded are fundamentally met privately in this respect."[9]

---

[8] Joe Trippi, *The Revolution Will Not Be Televised: Democracy, the Internet and the Overthrow of Everything* (New York: Regan Books, 2004), p. 235-6.

[9] Jeff Zeleny and and Michael Luo, "Public Financing? Obama and McCain Appear Split," *The New York Times*, April 10, 2008, *http://www.nytimes.com*; Transcript of The Diane Rehm Show, "Public Financing for the Presidential Campaign," Tuesday April 15, 2008 (Transcripts by Soft Scribe LLC). See also Thomas Cmar, "Toward a Small Donor Democracy: The Past and Future of Incentive Programs for Small Political Contributions," *Fordham Urban Law Journal*, Vol 32, no. 443 (2005) p. 151.

There are two issues here. The first is strictly empirical and is the subject of the current chapter. To what extent are these claims valid? Is it true that the funding of Obama's campaign represented something really different, replacing big donors with newly empowered small contributors? Has the country, at least at the presidential level, moved to a small donor democracy? The second issue concerns the content of a small donor funding system and whether it is the functional equivalent of a public funding system as the Obama campaign claimed. This latter question is reserved for the next chapter.

In assessing the importance of small and big donors it is important to take into account the critical role big donors play early in the electoral season, the period before the first primary elections. It is then that potential candidates seek to accumulate the funds necessary to establish their viability. Michael J. Malbin and Sean A. Cain write that, "before the first caucuses and primaries, the candidates (other than incumbents and front-runners) have a hard time differentiating themselves in the eyes of the general public (or potential small donors) from their same party opponents." The result is that newcomers and relative unknowns "depend financially on a thin layer of donors (and bundlers) who can supply them with checks of $1,000 or more."[10] Put another way, the early "wealth primary" is a contest among candidates for big investors. In this way those early large private donors are endowed with decision-making power over candidate viability.

The role of big donors in the wealth primary thus closely resembles the function of venture capitalists in the real economy. In the economy these are the investors who differentiate themselves from others because of their willingness to underwrite businesses before those firms have fully established their commercial profitability. They are risk-takers who invest in promising start-up firms. Once (and if) those start-up businesses become profitable, they often will seek to broaden their capital base by issuing new shares in the company through an initial public offering (IPO). Members of the public, often small investors, then become

---

[10] Michael J. Malbin and Sean A. Cain, *The Ups and Downs of Small and Large Donors*, p. 5.

part owners though almost never is a controlling interest in the firm made available. That power typically remains in the hands of the original investors, the ones who provided the money in the first place.

Table 3.5

Percentage of Contributions to Barack Obama's Presidential Campaign over Time and by Level of Contribution

Period	**Less than $200**	**More than $1,000**
2007		
First Quarter	22	68
Second Quarter	29	60
Third Quarter	28	54
Fourth Quarter	47	34
Total 2007	32	54
2008		
First Quarter	45	37
April	65	16
May	63	19
June	65	17

Source: Campaign Finance Institute, *Presidential Candidates' Fundraising Activities*, for selected time periods. http://www.cfinst.org.

The Obama campaign can be understood precisely in these terms. As indicated in Table 3.5, very early in his effort to secure the nomination of the

Democratic Party, 68 percent of his funding came from individual contributions in excess of $1,000. At that time, small donations provided only 22 percent of his financing. This was Obama's venture capital stage. Gradually through 2007 these percentages changed, with the relative importance of big donations falling and of small donations increasing. Even so however, through the end of 2007 more than half the funds collected by Obama and his bundlers came from large contributions; only about one-third came from small donations. The big change occurred in 2008, by which time Obama had come to be considered among the front runners. It was then that small payments became increasingly important to his campaign's financing. At the end of the first quarter of 2008, Obama reported that the amount received in small contributions exceeded that of large ones. During the second quarter of that year, donations of $200 or less represented about two-thirds of the funds flowing to his campaign.

These data are useful in identifying the importance of big contributions in getting Obama's campaign off the ground. Early on he relied on the funds provided by a relatively small number of big donors who were willing to invest in his campaign well before he became the front-runner. Only later, when his effort looked more likely to be a success, did small donors become important in his funding effort. It was not until April of 2008 that contributions of $200 or less became dominant.

But there is yet another reason to believe that the importance of small donors has been exaggerated. Such a distortion occurs because the reports to the FEC itemize contributions but do not identify donors. Each time a candidate receives a donation of $200 or less it is recorded as a discrete, separate gift, adding to the amount that seems to be raised in small contributions. But accounting for income in that way means that people who make more than one such small contribution are not identified. A donor who, for example, on five separate occasions during the course of the campaign makes a contribution of $200 is not identified as someone who provided $1,000, a large contribution.

Rather the campaign records five distinct small contributions. To the extent that Obama's campaign benefited from repeat contributions of under $200, the way the data are collected results in an overstatement of the importance of small contributors.

Michael J. Malbin of the Campaign Finance Institute has attempted to identify the importance of such repeat donations. The effort is to obtain a more accurate estimate of the amount of money that individual contributors provide to a campaign by adding together those repeat donations. Small donors in this exercise are only those individuals who in the aggregate provided $200 or less. Excluded from the small donor classification are those people who made multiple contributions which when added together exceeded $200.

The exclusion of repeat donors drastically reduces the estimated overall importance of small contributors to the Obama campaign. As indicated in Table 3.6, the revised estimate is that only 26 percent of the campaign funds came from small donors, compared to the 53 percent estimate that is obtained when multiple contributions are ignored.

Table 3.6

Estimates of Percentage Received by Obama Campaign by Level of Contribution, When Corrected for Multiple Contributions

	Not Corrected	Corrected
$200 or Less	53	26
$1,000 or More	29	47

Source: Michael J. Malbin, *Small Donors, Large Donors and the Internet: The Case of Public Financing after Obama* (Washington DC: The Campaign Finance Institute, 2009); Campaign Finance Institute, "CFI Retrospective analysis of 2008 Presidential Election campaign, January 8, 2010," Table 1.

The pattern in which big donors play an important role early in the primary election season but then experience a relative decline as the general election approaches, means that small donors in the political realm assume an analogous role to that of small shareholders in the economy. Their principal function is to provide capital. But they are not responsible for the financing that brings a candidate to the public's attention, nor are they present when the campaign's tactical and ideological trajectory is being established. In light of the fact that small donors gave only a relatively small proportion of Obama's early campaign funds it is hard to imagine that they could exercise a sufficient degree of influence to reverse policy commitments that the candidate had made to the venture capitalists – the big donors - early in his campaign.

What this suggests is that small donors play a distinctly subordinate role in the political process, even in a campaign such as Obama's which placed such stress on their importance. Their role pales when compared to the importance of big donors who provide the most funds and do so early in the electoral process. Notwithstanding the claims on its behalf by the Obama campaign, neither at the Congressional nor at the presidential level has the United States switched to a system of political finance that substantially empowers small donors at the expense of big contributors.

Chapter 4

Equality versus Small Donor Funding

With its 1976 Buckley v. Valeo decision the Supreme Court permitted the Federal Election Campaign Act's (FECA) restrictions on campaign contributions to come into force. In that same ruling, however, the Court struck down as unconstitutional FECA's limits on campaign expenditures. Both provisions raised what the justices called "fundamental First Amendment interests." They reasoned that constraints on political donations were acceptable if their intention was "to limit the actuality and appearance of corruption." However, the members of the Court argued that FECA's expenditure ceiling imposed "significantly more severe restrictions on protected freedoms of political expression and association than do its limitations on financial contributions." In the Court's view, expenditure limits were impermissibly intended to equalize "the relative ability of all voters to affect electoral outcomes." As the majority opinion put it, "the concept that government may restrict the speech of some elements of our society in order to enhance the relative voice of others is wholly foreign to the First Amendment...." Despite this ban, the Court in that same decision ruled that FECA's Presidential public funding system limiting expenditures to the amount provided by the government was constitutional. These restrictions did not violate the First Amendment, the Court argued, because the new system was voluntary. Since no one is compelled to accept public funding, the First Amendment is not violated.[1]

Because it barred anything other than a voluntary acceptance of limitations on campaign expenditures, the Buckley decision has widely been considered an

[1] "Buckley et al. v. Valeo,, Secretary of the United States Senate et al," 424 U.S. 1, http://www.epic.org/free_speech/buckley v valeo.html.

onerous obstacle to reforming the way electoral efforts are financed.[2] But in this regard, Michael J. Malbin makes the important point that "the Court has never questioned a legislature's ability to pursue campaign finance reform, so long as those methods do not limit speech."[3] Beyond curbing corruption, campaign finance reform might seek such goals as encouraging electoral competition or seeking to achieve greater citizen equality and participation in the political process. Indeed the Court made this point explicitly. In , the decision that validated most of the Bipartisan Campaign Reform Act (BCRA), the majority cited an earlier Court opinion that declared "to say that Congress is without power to pass appropriate legislation to safeguard…an election from the improper use of money to influence the result is to deny to the nation in a vital particular the power of self-protection."[4] Congress thus possesses a license to create a Congressional public funding system similar to that of the presidential system. To date however it has not legislated a reform that would embody the public goods attributes of the electoral process.

In contrast to the lack of action in Washington, a great deal of experimentation with various forms of voluntary public funding systems has occurred at the state and local level. Michael G. Miller reports that as of 2008 nearly half of the states possessed some form of public funding in at least one election. A full public funding option is available to candidates for New Mexico's Public Regulation Commission and the same is true for judicial candidates in that state as well as in Wisconsin and North Carolina.[5] The most important of these innovations has been adopted in Maine, Arizona and Connecticut, where full public funding is available to candidates for state offices. The first two of these

---

[2] See for example, Twentieth Century Fund/Century Foundation Working Group on Campaign Finance Litigation, *Buckley Stops Here*, Drafted by E. Joshua Rozenkranz (New York: The Century Foundation Press, 1998).

[3] Michael J. Malbin, "Rethinking the Campaign Finance Agenda," *The Forum*, Vol. 6, no 1 (2008), The Berkeley Electronic Press, Article 3, p. 7.

[4] Supreme Court of the United States, McConnell v. Federal Election Commission 540 U.S (2003), 118 http://www.lar.cornell. edu/supct/html/02-16/4.zs.html.

[5] Michael G. Miller, "Public Money, Candidate Time and Electoral Outcomes in State Legislative Elections," p. 2. http://www.nyaapor.org/pdfs/2008StudentPaperWinnerMiller.pdf?cff7f010.

states have had such "clean election" systems in place since 1996 and 1998 respectively, while Connecticut's legislature passed its public funding program in 2005. While it is too early to examine how the new system has changed politics in Connecticut, the record is extensive enough in Maine and Arizona to formulate at least an initial impression of its consequences there.

Not surprisingly, freed from the need to raise money from voluntary contributors, publicly funded office-seekers communicate more with their constituents than do privately funded candidates. Miller writes that "in both states, publicly funded candidates are able to devote significantly more time to voter mobilization efforts…."[6] Furthermore, Neil Mahlotra concludes that a public funding option increases electoral competition. With competitiveness measured as the number of effective candidates per race and the closeness of victory margins, Malhotra finds that in both Maine and Arizona public financing made "those races where challengers accepted [public] monies more competitive," a finding that holds both for open-seat contests and for those where an incumbent was running for re-election. In reviewing his statistical analysis, Malhotra concludes that "the empirical evidence on public financing suggests that these programs do not simply fill the coffers of unserious and low-quality candidates, but rather they help serious contestants mount effective challenges."[7]

In effect therefore, "clean elections" accomplishes the goal of making electoral contests more egalitarian and does so in a constitutionally acceptable way. Instead of limiting expenditures to achieve greater parity, it accomplishes that goal by making public funds available to candidates who might otherwise not be able to mount effective campaigns.

As a result, public financing has proved to be quite popular among politicians, particularly in Maine. As indicated in Table 4.1, in both of Maine's legislative assemblies between 70 and 85 percent of candidates run with public

---

[6] Ibid., p. 2.

[7] Neil Malhotra, "The Impact of Public Financing on Electoral Competition: Evidence from Arizona and Maine," *State Politics and Policy Quarterly*, Vol. 8, No. 3 (Fall 2008), p. 275, 277.

funds, and about 80 percent of election winners are publicly funded. The data are somewhat less impressive for Arizona but nonetheless provide evidence of the system's attractiveness as well as its effectiveness. While only about 30 percent of Arizona's Senate is "clean" it still remains the case that close to 60 percent of candidates for state-wide office are publicly funded and almost half of the seats in the House of Representatives were won by candidates who voluntarily agreed to eschew private funds. In both states it is clear that politicians have found public funding to be an effective means to run for office.

Table 4.1

Percent of Publicly Funded Candidates for Arizona and Maine Legislatures, 2006.

	Maine		**Arizona**	
	House	**Senate**	**House**	**Senate**
Primary Election Candidates	71.8	80.5	59.2	53.2
Primary Election Winners	80.9	89.2	61.2	56.0
General Election Candidates	78.1	85.7	60.9	54.9
General Election Winners	80.5	82.9	48.3	30.0

Source: *Breaking Free with Fair Elections: A New Declaration of Independence for Congress*, (N.P: Brennan Center for Justice, Common Cause, Democracy Matters, Public Campaign, Public Citizen, and U.S. PIRG, March 2007) p. 8-9.

In light of the successes experienced by full public funding in Arizona and Maine, it comes as a surprise that the campaign reform community has not coalesced around "clean elections" as its principle objective. The experiences in Arizona and Maine might have been viewed as successful pilot projects. As such they might have been employed as the basis upon which to scale up the same model for use at the national level. But though there are reform organizations and individuals who do advocate full public funding of Congressional campaigns, by no means is there unanimity in this regard.

Instead, an enhanced role for small donors in electoral campaigns has become the alternative of choice for a substantial body of reformers. As we have seen, Barack Obama became an enthusiastic supporter of small donor funding, despite the fact that as a Senator he had sponsored a full public campaign funding bill for Congressional candidates. Typically, small donor advocates do not suggest abandoning public subsidies altogether. Rather, they seek to enlarge the role of contributors who provide donations of less than $200, viewing these private funds as a supplement to public subsidies.

Leaving aside the empirical question taken up in Chapter 3 of how important small donors have in fact become, the question that arises is why a small donor system is so attractive to reformers.

One answer is provided by Mark Schmitt who writes that in recent years "there have been some tremendously positive developments in our politics." He reports that "the public is engaged with politics as never before," and that there has emerged "a true small-donor fund-raising base in both parties, a base driven more by ideas and passions about the direction of the country than by a desire for access to promote a particular interest." Schmitt would like to tap into and enhance the role of this small donor constituency.[8]

Schmitt argues further that "making political contributions is not something to be discouraged but a reasonable means of expressing 'intensity of desire.'" He writes, "imagine a hypothetical campaign financing system that gave every candidate who qualified for the ballot by signature an exactly equal amount

---

[8] Mark Schmitt, "Mismatching Funds: How Small-Donor Democracy Can Save Campaign Finance Reform," *Democracy: A Journal of Ideas*, Issue #4 (Spring 2007) *http://www.democracyjournal.org/article.php?ID=6516*. Differences in formatting make it impossible to provide pagination for quotations from this source in this and the following paragraph. The quotations in the following three paragraphs are taken from this source.

of funds and prohibited private funds; it would be chaotic and unrepresentative because it would strip this element of intensity of desire from the system." He goes on, "we all have one vote, but we have preferences of varying intensity, which politics should reflect."

Schmitt agrees that because income is unequally distributed, donations are "not a perfect way to sort out candidates." But, he adds, "we lack a better one that adequately reflects intensity." Schmitt sees the New York City public finance multiple-matching system as a way to advance the cause of small donors. For its municipal elections, New York provides $6 for every $1 raised by candidates from donors who provide $175 or less. This, in Schmitt's view, encourages small donors who feel strongly about their preferences to make political contributions. As he puts it, such a system "respect[s] the role of money as a legitimate expression of enthusiasm and a form of participation."

That Schmitt has made such a call is of particular significance since when he worked at the Open Society Institute, it was he who encouraged that foundation to contribute funds to "clean election" efforts such as those that succeeded in implementing full public funding systems in Maine and Arizona. But Schmitt now calls for the campaign reform community to "...revisit the principles on which it was founded."

Michael J. Malbin too believes that a small donor system should be adopted, but arrives at this conclusion differently than Schmitt. He does so because on one hand he is dubious about the viability of "clean elections" systems, and on the other hand he believes that a small donor system would be effective in offsetting the distortions that result from the dominance of big donations.

Malbin's skepticism about "clean elections" rests on his view that the abandonment of the presidential public funding system during the 2007-08 election cycle revealed a flaw in the system more fundamental than merely the fact that too little money was available in it. This more profound problem, he believes, centers on the difficulty of setting the appropriate level of publicly funded political expenditures. Malbin writes, "the problem is in knowing at what level a limit is 'realistic' in a specific election context." If the limit is set too high, the system is wasteful. If however it is set too low, candidates will not participate, as has occurred with the presidential funding system. This conundrum is compounded by the fact that a recent Supreme Court decision has put in doubt the constitutionality of increasing public funding for candidates faced with opponents who are extravagantly financed from private sources.[9] The consequence, Malbin writes, is that "eventually any policy designer (and candidate) will have to face up to the spending limits" imposed by public funding. He is concerned that those spending limits will mean that candidates, as Barack Obama did in 2008, will opt out of the public funding system, particularly if a privately funded candidate is able to raise contributions in excess of the level available to a "clean" candidate. Rather than leave this problem unresolved, Malbin wants to fill the funding gap with small donors. Doing so could both offset the "representational distortion" caused by big donors and also avoid the problem of limited public funding.[10]

In support of his argument that an enhanced role for small donors will dilute the power of big contributors Malbin cites a preliminary report on the results of a Campaign Finance Institute (CFI) survey of candidates for state office in six states and of donors and non-donors in seven states. The CFI study found that "small donors differ from large donors in important ways" and that "in some instances, the policy views of small donors corresponded more closely with those of non-donors than of large donors." On this basis, the study concludes that

---

[9] The Supreme Court invalidated the "millionaire" amendment to BCRA which tripled the amount of money a publicly funded candidate could raise when a self-financed opponent exceeded a stipulated level of expenditures, but left unchanged the contributions the latter could receive. See Supreme Court of the United States, Davis v. Federal Election Commission, No. 07-320.

[10] Michael J. Malbin, *Small Donors, Large Donors and the Internet: The Case for Public Financing after Obama*, (Washington DC: The Campaign Finance Institute, April 2009), p. 19-20.

increasing the role of small donors represents a means by which to offset big donor domination.[11]

Thus while Malbin believes that candidates should be provided with a public grant, he thinks that they should also be allowed to raise supplementary funds, but with the caveat that those funds should come only from small donors. He proposes, that is, a hybrid system. In this way he writes, "the system could...be redesigned to foster participation by small donors and reduce candidates' dependence on large donors." To this end, he cites funding systems proposed by reform organizations including the American Civil Liberties Union and Democracy 21. These systems contain a provision by which a publicly financed candidate faced with an opponent who exceeds a specified level of expenditures will be able to raise unlimited amounts of money at least some of which would be with matched public funds.[12]

The Fair Elections Now Act (FENA) submitted to Congress in 2009 by Senators Richard Durbin and Arlen Specter in the Senate and Representatives John Larson and Walter Jones in the House of Representatives proposes such a hybrid approach and goes even further in enhancing the role of small donors than is typically advocated by promoters of this approach. The Congressional bill calls for participating candidates to receive a basic public grant, and also provides a four to one match for donations of $100 or less - the maximum individual donation candidates may receive – up to a specific level. Beyond this, office-seekers would be free to receive any number of donations of no more than $100, but these will not generate a public match.[13]

In assessing the idea that small donors should be encouraged, the first point that should be made is that the hybrid model represents abandonment of the

---

[11] Wesley Y. Joe, Michael J. Malbin, Clyde Wilcox, Peter W. Brusoe and Jamie P. Pimlott, *Do Small Donors Improve Representation? Some Answers from Recent Gubernatorial and State Legislative Elections*, (Washington DC: Campaign Finance Institute 2008), p. 3, 16.

[12] Ibid. p. 20.

[13] *http://www.fairelectionsnow.org*. FENA's content is subject to negotiation and change, and as a result Malbin's exposition, which omits this last clause, is at the time of this writing, August 9, 2009,out of date.

principle that the electoral system should be treated as a public good. Rather, in the name of reform, it would strengthen the role of selected investors, albeit in this case small investors. It is true that only an attenuated version of the public goods principle is present in the voluntary "clean elections" systems that the Supreme Court has found acceptable. The Court has ruled that publicly funded candidacies must only be an available option, not the sole means available to run for office. Candidates, if they choose to do so, must possess the option of securing private funding. But the popularity of the "clean elections" model in the states in which it has been implemented means that in practice something very close to elections as a public good is practiced. The widespread participation in the system in both Arizona and Maine suggests that in those states the role of private financing has been substantially minimized, though not entirely eliminated. With this the case, the hybrid model represents a substantial retreat. Its enhancement of the financing role of small donors falls short of the equality embedded in the treatment of elections as a public good.

Second, there is a serious problem with Schmitt's claim that a small donor system is desirable because it provides a vehicle for political passion. His argument overlooks the fact there are a variety of ways commitment can be expressed that, because they do not privilege wealth, are preferable to donations. Politically passionate people can become personally involved by canvassing, organizing meetings, or arranging political house parties. All represent involvement; the more passionate, the more a person will engage in such activities. Schmitt is right that commitment is important in politics and that avenues should be made available for its expression. But he does not accord sufficient weight to the fact that political volunteering provides such a vehicle. Since there is literally no limit to the extent that a person can express passion by donating time to campaign organizations, it is both unnecessary and undesirable to assign a special role to donations as an expression of commitment. Doing so involves an acceptance of economic inequality in democracy, a system that should be protected from the power of wealth.

There are grounds to doubt, furthermore, that the promoting of small donations will spill over and result in a substantial increase in political volunteerism. Survey data indicate that about 8 percent of the population make political contributions though Malbin believes this figure, small as it is, probably is an overstatement.[14] What is significant in the current context, however, is the fact that in a survey of voters in the 2004 presidential election, only 6 percent of donors who made a political contribution of $100 or less reported volunteering in elections.[15] Promoters of internet-donating point to the fact that small online donors are more politically active than small offline contributors. On that basis they argue like Schmitt for the use of the internet to advance both small donations and thereby more direct political activism. But that same survey data indicate that only 26 percent of online small donors attended even one house party during the 2004 campaign. By way of comparison, 40 percent of donors who contributed $500 or more online did so. Similarly, while only 15 percent of offline small donors attended these informal gatherings, 37 percent of offline big donors participated in them.[16] What these data suggest is that an enhanced role for small donors may increase political activism, but the extent to which it will offset the role of big donors is likely to be quite small.

Third, Malbin overstates the case against "clean elections" with his argument concerning the problems associated with setting contribution and spending limits. He is not wrong that an expenditure limit is an integral part of a public funding system and that that limit should be set at an equilibrium level. It should not be higher than the level needed to attract politicians to the system but not so low as to dissuade office-seekers from participation. And further, he is

---

[14] Michael J. Malbin, "Rethinking the Campaign Finance Agenda," p. 9.

[15] Institute for Politics Democracy & the Internet, in Collaboration with the Campaign Finance Institute, *Small Donors and Online Giving: A Study of Donors to the 2004 Presidential Campaigns* (Washington DC: The George Washington University, March 2006), p. 33.

[16] Ibid. p. 33.

right that the equilibrium will vary according to circumstance. But none of this necessarily leads to a determination that an equilibrium level of expenditures cannot be achieved or at least approximated in practice, though he uses this conclusion to justify abandoning full public funding. Certainly the failure of the presidential funding system does not require that judgment.

The only adjustments that have been made in presidential public funding since FECA was passed in 1974 have been those associated with the inflation rate. In "real" terms there has been no increase at all. This stagnation has occurred despite the greatly increased use of expensive television advertising and long distance travel in political campaigns. The presidential system was abandoned by candidates because needed financial level adjustments have not been attempted, not because they were tried and failed.

Indeed Malbin himself points out that precisely the kind of adjustments that a viable public funding system requires has periodically and successfully been implemented in Minnesota.[17] Similarly the very high rates at which candidates participate in the "clean election" systems in Arizona and Maine indicate that the task of setting appropriate spending limits is not as difficult as Malbin suggests. These favorable outcomes at the state level indicate that the presidential system's failure occurred because the need for fine-tuning was neglected when the system was constructed by Congress, and not as Malbin implies because of the inherent difficulty of identifying the level appropriate for presidential candidates. Clearly, Malbin overstates the problem with expenditure limits.

But fourth and perhaps most importantly is the extent to which the problem of representational distortion would be overcome by the hybrid model. This issue can be examined by looking at the demographic composition of small donors. In particular it is important to try to learn the extent to which the social composition of small donors corresponds to that of the population as a whole. If

[17] Michael J. Malbin, *Small Donors, Large Donors and the Internet*, p. 19.

there were a substantial degree of overlap in incomes and earnings between the two, then allowing small donors to assume the funding role that would otherwise be filled by the public sector would not cause a substantial degree of political bias. If the opposite were the case however, the enhancement of the role of small donors relative to public funding would be associated with a loss in representational equality.

The best data available to study this issue are in the CFI study of 2006 state elections mentioned earlier and in the survey of voters undertaken in 2004 by the Institute for Politics, Democracy & the Internet (IPDI) cited above. What makes the study of this issue difficult is the fact that campaign contributions of less than $200 do not have to be itemized in the reports candidates provide to the FEC. However, candidates in primary elections are required to provide the FEC with information concerning the contributions that the government is committed to matching. Response to this requirement provides the bulk of the database for the 2004 presidential election study. It surveyed 935 individuals who either had contributed to the six Democrats participating in the primary publicly financed election matching system, or to Ralph Nader. In addition, the IPDI survey included individuals about whom information had been provided by the Bush/Cheney campaign.[18] In both studies, small donors were those who contributed $100 or less to a candidate during an election cycle.

Data from the two studies make it quite clear that if there were a shift away from big donors to small donors the new funders would still be unrepresentative of the population generally. Tables 4.2 and 4.3 compare the income distribution of small donors with the distribution of income for all United States households. The income classifications in the two tables are not identical so it is not possible directly to compare the presidential and congressional experiences. Similarly the income cut-offs used in the states study are not the

[18] Institute for Politics, Democracy and the Internet, *Small Donors and Online Giving: A Study of Donors to the 2004 Presidential Campaigns,* p. 8. Though these are the best data available on the national level, legitimate questions can be raised about the representative nature of this sample since the CFI study did not have access to information from the Kerry and Dean campaigns.

same as those used by the federal government in reporting incomes. Nevertheless the pattern is clear. Among small donors, low income people are underpresented relative to their size in the population.

Table 4.2

Income Distribution: Small Donors to 2004 Presidential Political Campaigns and United States Households

Income Level	**Donors**	**U.S. Households**
Less than $25,000	8	28
$25,000-49,999	21	27
$50,000-99,999	38	29
Above $100,000	33	16

Source: Institute for Politics, Democracy and the Internet, *Small Donors and Online Giving: A Study of Donors to the 2004 Presidential Campaigns,* Table 2; U.S. Households; Calculated from U.S. Census Bureau, *Statistical Abstract of the United States 2007* (Washington DC: Government Printing Office, 2006), Table 671.

Table 4.3

Income Distribution: Small Donor Contributors at State Level 2006 and U.S. Population 2005

Income Level	Donors	2005 Income	Population
Less than $40,000	11.2	Under 35,000	38.5
$40-75000	25.4	35-75,000	33.3
75000 +	63.3	75,000+	28.6

Source: Campaign Finance Institute, *Do Small Donors Improve Representation?*, Table 1 and U.S. Bureau of the Census *Statistical Abstract of the United States 2008,* (Washington: Government Printing Office, 2007), Table 219

In the presidential race (Table 4.2) only 8 percent of small donors earned $25,000 or less, though 28 percent of households in the country generally fell into that income category. And while 29 percent of small donors earned under $50,000, the proportionate share of American households earning that level of income was almost twice as large – 55 percent. The same pattern of under-representation of low income people among small donors was present at the state level (Table 4.3). While 11.2 percent of small donors at the state level earned less than $40,000, 38.5 percent of the United States population had annual earnings of about that level (under $35,000). Almost two-thirds of small donors (63.3 percent) earned more than $75,000, while only about one-quarter of United States households (28.6 percent) earned at least that much. Small donors are more affluent than the American population taken as a whole.

Table 4.4

Levels of Educational Attainment of Small Donors to Presidential Political Campaigns and United States Population, 2004

Education Attainment	Small Donors	U.S. Population
Less than College Degree	24	72
Bachelor's Degree	25	18
Advanced Degree	52	10

[1] College Degree and Some Graduate School.
Source: Institute for Politics, *Democracy and the Internet, Small Donors and Online Giving,* Table 2; U.S. Population: Calculated from U.S. Census Bureau, *Statistical Abstract of the United States, 2007,* Table 216.

The relatively privileged status of small donors is corroborated when their educational attainment is compared to that of the population taken as a whole (Tables 4.4 and 4.5). While 10 percent of the American people in 2004 had

Table 4.5

Distribution of Levels of Educational Attainment: Small Donors at State Level 2006 and U.S. Population 2005

Education Attainment	Percent Donors	2005 Percent Population
Less than College Degree	27.3	71.9
Bachelor	27.9	18.3
Advanced Degree	44.7	9.7

Source: Campaign Finance Institute, *Do Small Donors Improve Representation?*, Table 1; *Statistical Abstract of the United States, 2008*, Table 219.

achieved an advanced degree, such individuals represented more than half (52 percent) of small donors to that year's presidential campaigns. At the state level, a very similar discrepancy is present. In the six states, 9.7 percent of the population had secured an advanced degree, but contributors with that level of education represented 44.7 percent of small donors. Small donors then have higher incomes and are better educated than typical Americans. Because this is so their interests are not identical with those of the American people. Empowering small donors would, as a result, accord an atypical group a privileged political status. Of course an increased role for small donors would result in a more egalitarian system than the one we possess at present. But it would be far from a democracy in which all individuals have an equal opportunity to exercise influence and find a political outlet for their ideas and passions. The risk that a small donor system represents is that in the name of replacing one form of donor elitism it would introduce a different form of the same phenomenon. Instead of the very wealthy dominating, political power would accrue to the relatively wealthy.

Chapter 5

The Crisis of Climate Change

Curbing the power of special interests has been a political preoccupation in the United States since the time of the American Revolution. In Federalist Paper Number 10, James Madison argued that the need to control special interests, or what he called factions, was central to the success of a representative political system. He wrote that a "friend of popular governments never finds himself so much alarmed for their character and fate as when he contemplates their propensity to this dangerous vice." Madison believed that "a manufacturing interest, a mercantile interest, a moneyed interest, with many less interests grow up of necessity in civilized nations." But because of the danger to the common good that they represent, "the regulation of these various and interfering interests forms the principal task of modern legislation."[1]

Madison wrote that "among the numerous advantages promised by a well constructed Union, none deserves to be more accurately developed than its tendency to break and control the violence of faction." Both Madison and his fellow authors of the Federalist Papers, Alexander Hamilton and John Jay, believed the new constitution then under consideration did this effectively. Under it, the "mischief" that a minority faction could inflict on society would be controlled. "Relief," wrote Madison, "…is supplied by the republican principle, which enables the majority to defeat its sinister views by regular vote." To be sure, a faction may "clog the administration, it may convulse the society; but it

---

[1] Quotations in this and the next two paragraphs are taken from the Library of Congress, *The Federalist Papers, Federalist No. 10*, "The Same Subject Continued: The Union as a Safeguard Against Domestic Faction and Insurrecton," November 23, 1787, http://thomas.loc.gov/home/histdox/fed_10.html.

will be unable to execute and mask its violence under the forms of the Constitution."

Madison himself worried about factions that we would today describe as residing on the political left: those that possessed "a rage for paper money, for an abolition of debts, for an equal division of property or for any other improper or wicked project." But in fact it is corporate based special interests that at present exercise disproportionate influence. Cass R. Sunstein, in his positive assessment of the Federalist Papers, nevertheless concedes that Madison and his colleagues were excessively sanguine concerning democracy's ability to neutralize the power of wealth. He writes that "one of the enduring challenges" to Madison's optimism lies in the fact that today "factions are able to exert their will, ensuring, for example, that legislation nominally designed to reduce air pollution or to enact insurance reform may in some respects reflect the influence of strong private interests."[2]

The fact is that the system by which we fund electoral campaigns functions in a way that empowers wealthy "factions." On one hand, running for a seat in the House of Representatives or the Senate becomes ever more expensive. On the other hand, the pool of large political donors remains only a small minority of the population. By possessing a choke-hold on the viability of candidates therefore, political contributors gain the ability to exercise leverage over the political process. And as Sunstein suggests, this power is used to achieve specific legislative outcomes beneficial to or at least consistent with donor interests.

In the next three chapters I examine how such factions have incapacitated our political system. They have hamstrung our ability to contend with global climate change and stymied efforts to construct a health care system that efficiently serves the needs of the American people. Similarly, Wall Street's money-backed political clout was central to the process of financial deregulation

---

[2] Cass R. Sunstein, "The Enlarged Republic – Then and Now," *The New York Review of Books*, March 26, 2009, p. 48.

that gave rise to the most severe economic downturn since the Depression of the 1930s. The problem that Madison and the Federalists identified is still with us, and just as they anticipated it continues to inflict "instability, injustice, and confusion."[3]

With regard to global climate change, we confront an exquisite contradiction that our political system has been unable successfully to address. Modern economic development is spreading globally, raising income levels and reducing poverty at rates never before seen in human experience. But that very growth has created a process of climate change that threatens to be so injurious that it will at least in some locations more than offset the gains associated with modernization. The energy sources that fuel modernization – particularly petroleum and coal – threaten to undo the very progress to which they were such important contributors.

No one foresaw this. Global warming was not even recognized as a threat until the beginning of the 1980s, just at the moment that the growth process was accelerating in Asia. It represents precisely the kind of problem that the economist Simon Kuznets elaborated on when, in his 1972 Nobel Prize address, he argued that negative unintended consequences were integral to the process of modern economic growth. According to Kuznets, "all economic growth brings some unexpected results in its wake, positive as well as negative, with the latter taking on greater importance as the mass effects of major innovations are felt and the needs that they are meant to satisfy are met."[4]

Kuznets uses as an example the increase in mortality that accompanied the industrial revolutions of the late 18th and early 19th century. Urban death rates were higher than those in the countryside. Rudimentary urban sanitation and water supply facilities in cities meant that their residents were more exposed to infectious diseases than those in rural areas. Thus life expectancy in London in

---

[3] The Library of Congress, *The Federalist Papers, Federalist No. 10.*

[4] Simon Kuznets, "Modern Economic Growth: Findings and Reflections," in Simon Kuznets, *Population, Capital and Growth* (New York: W.W. Norton & Company Inc., 1973), p. 174, 176.

1841 was only 35 years, 25 in Liverpool, and 24 in Manchester. But in the rural county of Surrey it was 44. As people relocated to urban areas in response to industrial employment opportunities, overall mortality rates tended to increase.[5]

The point to be made in this regard, however, is that it was not necessary to renounce and reverse growth to solve the problems that development had caused. Declining mortality occurred in the second half of the 19th century in Europe and North America largely as a result of the same kind of innovative behavior that gave rise to modernization in the first place. Urban mortality rates were reduced when improved public health measures affecting water quality, waste disposal, paved roads, food supply and personal hygiene significantly diminished the toxicity of urban life.[6]

Seen in this perspective, global climate change represents, much like rising mortality in the early stages of the growth process, collateral damage – the negative unintended effect of the progress associated with modern economic growth. Just as infectious diseases had to be brought under control in the 19th century to allow urban-based economic growth to advance, today carbon dioxide and other greenhouse gas emissions must be minimized in order to allow global economic development and the eradication of poverty to proceed without devastating climatic effects. The task that confronts contemporary society with regard to global climate change, as was the case in the 19th century with regard urban death rates, is to mobilize an effective response that both solves the problem and permits continued economic growth.

But the challenges caused by high urban death rates and global climate change differ as well. The most important is their scale. In both the source of the problem and its impact, the global climate change problem dwarfs the urban mortality issue, confined as the latter was to geographically circumscribed areas

---

[5] Michael R. Haines, "Conditions of Work and the Decline of Mortality," in Roger Schofield and David Reher, "The Decline in Mortality in Europe," in R. Schofield, D. Reher and A. Bideau (eds.) *The Decline in Mortality in Europe* (Oxford: Clarendon Press, 1991), p. 179-180.

[6] Richard A. Easterlin, *Growth Triumphant: The Twenty-First Century in Historical Perspective* (Ann Arbor: The University of Michigan Press, 1996), p. 79.

in a relatively few countries. Today, though just a handful of countries are responsible for the bulk of greenhouse gas emissions, all regions of the world contribute to the problem. And though some regions will be harmed more than others, none will be immune to its negative consequences.

It is tempting to argue that the problems caused by the extensive use of greenhouse gas-emitting fossil fuels are principally the result of market failure and that overcoming that failure will be sufficient to correct the problem. And in fact, as things stand today, neither consumers nor producers are asked to pay for the full cost of the use of coal and petroleum. There is market failure. The environmental costs of using fossil fuels are externalized – taking the form either of environmental degradation or of taxpayers paying for clean-up efforts. With this the case it might be thought that if consumers and producers were required to pay the full costs associated with the use of these energy sources, firms would shift away from their use and employ alternative, less environmentally damaging fuels.

This is the logic that motivates advocates of a carbon tax or a cap and trade system. In the first, there would be a government-imposed financial penalty for the use of coal or petroleum, much as cigarette smokers incur such a penalty when they buy that product. With a cap and trade system, an increase in producer costs would also result. With this approach an overall national cap on emissions would be established, with individual firms assigned a specific permissible amount of such pollutants. Firms able to produce with emissions lower than their permitted level would be free to sell their unused allotment to firms that exceed theirs. The purchase price of the right to emit would increase the production costs of the firm buying the permit. This increase would act as an incentive for firms to identify and utilize more environmentally-friendly technologies.

The problem is that correcting the market failure in either of these ways is socially very costly. An increase in energy costs means that the gains achieved in emissions controls will come at the expense of lost output, consumption and employment. With higher production costs, economic activity will be reduced, at least potentially putting upward pressure on unemployment and poverty rates.

To be successful without causing economic damage, either a carbon tax or a cap and trade system requires a technological complement. Alternative energy sources have to be available at prices that are low enough so that their adoption will not substantially raise the costs of production. An effective approach to global climate change therefore requires that both sides of the problem be addressed simultaneously. While the costs of fossil fuels have to be raised, at the same time alternative technologies must be made available so that phasing out coal and petroleum will not cause an economic calamity. The brutal fact however is that to date the technologies associated with wind power, solar power, bio-fuels, geo-power and the capturing and storing of carbon dioxide emissions have not advanced sufficiently to make them cost-effective substitutes for coal and petroleum.

Among the alternatives, nuclear power comes closest to representing a viable alternative. It does not create carbon dioxide emissions and therefore promises to allow continued economic growth without contributing to climate change. Three problems however stand in the way of its replacing fossil fuels. The first concerns safety. This has been a particular worry since the accidents at Three Mile Island and Chernobyl. Second is the problem caused by the radioactive waste that is produced by nuclear energy. At the moment that waste is stored at sites close to the plants themselves, with the anticipation that ultimately it will be relocated to more secure locations deep underground. Uncertainty about the disposition of this dangerous material raises the question of whether it represents an unforeseen externalized cost, much as greenhouse gases did. Although there is the hope that advanced technology will allow this material to be reprocessed, at the moment that solution does not exist.

The third issue is profitability. The problem here stems from the very high cost of constructing a nuclear energy facility. It is this, more than the public's concerns over safety and waste disposal, that is responsible for the fact that in most countries nuclear power remains a minor source of energy. Globally in 2005, nuclear power provided only about 16 percent of world energy production.[7] Indeed, in the United States the number of nuclear operating units has declined from 112 to 104.[8] A detailed academic study of the issue concludes that a big increase in nuclear power is unlikely. The authors write, "high capital cost, uncertain construction cost and potential construction and licensing delays are likely to lead private investors to require a substantial risk premium over coal and gas fired power plants to finance at least the first new nuclear units." As they put it "despite recent revived interest in nuclear power, the prospects for merchant nuclear investment in liberalized industries without government support do not seem promising."[9]

Until the inauguration of Barack Obama, the issue of global climate change had not been high on either Congressional or Presidential agendas. It is true that in response to the petroleum crises of the 1970s, the United States government did dramatically increase its funding for research and development in renewable energy sources (Table 5.1). The budget for such research, adjusted for inflation, reached a peak of over $1 billion between 1977 and 1981. But thereafter the Department of Energy's budget for research in renewable fossil and nuclear energy declined dramatically. By 1990 93 it stood at a level of about $180 million, an 85 percent fall from its peak. Though there was a gradual upward trend in the budget for this research in the years thereafter, by 2006-08 it still totaled only $374 million, less that 32 percent of its earlier high water mark. Obviously, the government did not sustain the kind of budgetary commitment that would have been required for renewable energy technology to become a viable

[7] R.E.H. Simms et al, "Energy Supply" in *Climate Change 2007 – Mitigation of Climate Change, Working Group III Contribution the Fourth Assessment Report of the Intergovernmental Panel on Climate Change 2007*, (New York: Cambridge University Press, 2007) p. 268.
[8] Energy Information Administration, *Monthly Energy Review*, June 2008, Table 8.1.
[9] Fabien A. Roques, William J. Nutall, David M. Newbery and Richard de Neufville, "Nuclear Power: A Hedge Against Uncertain Gas and Carbon Prices," *The Energy Journal*, Vol. 27, no. 4 (October 2006), p. 20.

alternative to fossil fuels. The result not surprisingly is that the country remained addicted to carbon dioxide-intensive sources of energy. As the Government Accountability Office puts it "the nation's energy portfolio has not dramatically changed - fossil energy today provides 85 percent of the nation's energy compared to 93 percent in 1973."[10]

Table 5.1

United States Government Research and Development Budgets for Renewable Energy Sources, 1974-2008 ($ millions in 2008 prices)

Years	$ millions
1974	35,656
1975-76	212,725
1977-81	1,203,312
1982-85	485,061
1986-89	266,688
1990-93	182,064
1994-97	295,933
1998-01	298,023
2002-05	277,825
2006-08	373,512

Source: Computed from International Energy Agency, Data Services, http://wds.iea.org/WDS/TableViewer/tableView.aspx.

This pattern of research neglect is testimony to the power of wealth in the political process. The absence of effort on the energy technology front is not traceable to public hostility on the subject but rather to the fact that the proponents of renewable energy have not been able to pay their way onto the political agenda. Polling data on the subject consistently finds that Americans support efforts to develop alternative energy-producing technologies. Data from a 2007 study indicate that 65 percent of Americans agree that the government should be

[10] United States Government Accountability Office, *Advanced Energy Technologies: Budget Trends and Challenges for DOE's Energy R&D Program*, March 5, 2008, http://www/gao.gov/new.items/d08556t.pdf.

"starting a major research effort costing up to $30 billion per year to develop new sources of energy." Gallup also found 81 percent supporting proposals for "spending more government money on developing solar and wind power." Taken as a whole these responses suggest, according to Joseph Carroll, that "in terms of what the government should be doing, the public supports major research efforts to develop new energy sources."[11]

Over and against this support for energy innovation is the fact that traditional energy industries have used their wealth politically. As indicated in Table 5.2 throughout the years since 1990 (the earliest year for which data are available) individuals associated with the oil and gas and electrical utilities industries – the industries with the greatest vested interest in petroleum and coal – donated vastly more money to Congressional office-seekers than did environmentalists and people associated with alternative energy production and services. Though the $27.0 million contributed by the latter seems like a great deal of money, it is trivialized by the $376.3 million that came from the proponents of petroleum and coal. This imbalance in contributions existed among Democrats as well as Republicans, though to a lesser degree.

However, the advent of the Obama administration brought with it the promise that the problem of global warming might for the first time be addressed. Knowing Obama's attitude toward environmental policy, the traditional fossil fuel users provided very little funding to his presidential campaign. The $2.7 million they donated is insignificant compared to the contributions of big donors - $43.7 million made by lawyers and lobbyists, the $39. 5 million provided by the finance, insurance and real estate (FIRE) sector, and the $25.5 million donated by communications/electronics.[12]

---

[11] This paragraph is based on American Environics, *Energy Attitudes: An Analysis of Opinion Research on Energy and Global Warming*, (American Environics, 2007), p. 14.
[12] Center for Responsive Politics, "Barack Obama: Industries," http://www.opensecrets.org.

Table 5.2

Federal Campaign Contributions by Selected Sector, 1990-2010[1] ($ millions)

	Total	To Democrats	To Republicans
Electrical Utilities	134.5	52.5	82.0
Oil and Gas	241.8	58.0	183.8
Total	376.3	110.5	265.8
Environmentalists	22.2	20.2	2.0
Alternative Energy	4.8	3.2	1.6
Total	27.0	23.4	3.0

[1] Data for 2010 election cycle as released by the Federal Election Commission, August 9, 2009. Source: Center for Responsive Politics, "Totals by Sector," http://www.opensecrets.org.

Reflecting this, Obama's administration came into office assigning a high priority to the problem of greenhouse gas emissions. In a speech at the annual meeting of the National Academy of Sciences in April 2009, President Obama declared that "our future on this planet depends on our willingness to address the challenge posed by carbon pollution" and that "energy is our great project, this generation's great project."[13] It was in this speech that Obama announced that his administration would increase public funding for research in renewable energy sources, and that in addition it would pursue "comprehensive legislation to place a market-based cap on carbon emissions," – a cap and trade system.

But while the Obama Administration made its intentions clear, it quickly learned that it is one thing to announce a goal and yet an entirely different matter to secure the Congressional legislation necessary to achieve that objective. As of this writing only the House of Representatives (but not the Senate) has passed a cap and trade system. And as described by John M. Broder in *The New York Times*, that legislation was "a patchwork of compromises" that fell "short of what many European governments and environmentalists have said is needed to avert

[13] The White House, Office of the Press Secretary, "Remarks by the President at the National Academy of Sciences Annual Meeting," April 27, 2009. http://www.whitehouse.gov.

the worst effects of global warming." In order to secure its passage, Broder explained, "the bill's targets for emissions of heat-trapping gases were weakened, its mandate for renewable electricity was scaled back, and incentives for industries were sweetened."[14]

At the same time, the new administration also tussled with Congress over spending for new environmental initiatives. For example, the Energy Secretary, Steven Chu, requested that $280 million be spent to create eight new research and development labs to work on clean energy solutions, but the House bill funding the Energy Department included only $35 million for that project. Similarly, though the administration proposed that $115 million be spent on a program called "Regaining our ENERGY Science and Engineering Edge (RE-ENERGYSE)," designed to pay for educational initiatives in energy science and engineering, that program was entirely eliminated in the Senate Energy and Water Appropriations Bill.[15]

While, in short, the Obama administration represented a much-needed change in the priority accorded to environmental issues, the Congress remained resistant. Initiatives were only grudgingly forthcoming and their size was far less than the problem called for, representing only scaled-down versions of ideas that had been suggested from within the environmental community. The Re-ENERGYSE program offered by the administration, for example, was much less ambitious than the National Energy Education Act proposed by the Breakthrough Institute upon which it was modeled. The original idea, if enacted, would have provided federal investments "to retool our nation's top universities and colleges as centers of research, education and workforce training in energy-related fields."[16] As such it was far bolder than anything the Obama Administration placed on the agenda for consideration or that Congress seriously considered.

---

[14] John M. Broder, "House Passes Bill to Address Threat of Climate Change," *The New York Times*, June 27, 2009. http://nytimes.com.

[15] Bryan Walsh, "Clean Energy: U.S. Lags in Research and Development," *Time*, August 1, 2009, http://www.time.com.

[16] Breakthrough Institute, "National Energy Education Act," www.thebreakthrough.org.

The bottleneck in Congress exists because, as Bryan Walsh has written in *Time* magazine, "the tiny renewable–power industry has little weight in Washington."[17] The proponents of renewable energy still have not been able to buy political clout in Washington DC. It remains the case that the traditional industries contribute much more to Congressional candidates than the advocates of new technologies, though the gap between the two has somewhat narrowed (Table 5-3). What has changed however is that the traditional energy industries have rebalanced their contributions between the parties. In contrast to the past, the electric utilities now provide almost as much funding to Democrats as to Republicans. The result is that during the 2008 election cycle and notwithstanding the fact that Obama was at the head of the ticket, Democrats received almost three times more money from the fossil fuel-intensive industries than they did from environmentalists and their industry allies ($18.0 million compared to $6.7 million). A deep bi-partisan bias, fueled by campaign contributions, against renewable energy thus continues in the Congress.

The fact that environmentalists provide almost no funding to Republicans reflects both the antipathy of members of that party to the Green movement and the fact that the latter has pinned its hopes on Democrats becoming will be receptive to their cause. Thus alternative-energy advocates Ted Nordhaus and Michael Shellenberger write: "the time is ripe for the Democratic party to embrace a new story about America." They argue that solving the problem of global climate change should be an important element in that narrative.[18]

---

[17] Bryan Walsh, "Clean Energy: U.S.Lags in Research and Development" *Time*, August 1, 2009, http://www.time.com.

[18] Ted Nordhaus and Michael Shellenberger, *Break Through: From the Death of Environmentalism to the Politics of Possibility* (Boston and New York: Houghton Mifflin Company, 2007), p. 13, 257-60.

Table 5.3

Federal Campaign Contribution to Democrats and Republicans by Selected Sector, 2008 ($ millions)

	Total	To Democrats	To Republicans
Electric Utilities	20.7	9.9	10.8
Oil & Gas	35.4	8.1	27.3
Total	56.1	18.0	38.1
Environmentalists	5.6	5.3	0.3
Alternative Energy Production and Services	1.9	1.4	0.5
Total	7.5	6.7	0.8

Source: See Table 5.2

But the experience of Obama's Democratic administration suggests that grounds for optimism in this regard are not secure. There is no doubt about the need. But because Democrats receive massive funding from fossil fuel users, they have shown themselves to be less than reliable in supporting the programs and funding on a scale that corresponds to the magnitude of the problem.

The reality is that what is required is a huge level of public research and development investment with regard to renewable energy. Such an effort will necessarily take the side of new and potential start-up firms against the entrenched interests of already-existing large corporations in the fossil fuel-using industries. The latter will continue to resist. One of their most powerful tools is to make some of their wealth available to the campaigns of politicians who side with them. The decision about an investment program in alternative energy technologies is necessarily a political and legislative one. People associated with the coal and petroleum industries can be expected to persist in their effort to influence both the composition of the Congress, and how members vote on this issue. The success the coal and petroleum industries have had in applying the brakes to Obama's environmental agenda is precisely what we can anticipate in our "pay to play" political system.

The struggle to develop non-polluting energy will therefore have to extend beyond normal partisan politics. Confronting the power of private wealth to shape the policies that emerge from the political process is critical, no matter which party holds the presidency or is dominant in the Congress. It is possible to offset environmental damage without consigning the poor to permanent penury. But the way forward will require a political movement able to overcome the formidable ability of wealthy special interests to block change.

Chapter 6

The Crisis of the Economy

Efficient financial markets are required for the real economy of production and employment to function successfully. When the financial system works well, banks and other similar institutions attract savings and lend those funds to businesses and consumers. With borrowed money, producers are able to purchase more buildings and equipment, and consumers more goods and services than they would be able to in the absence of credit. Since this is so, a disruption in financial markets has the potential to cause great damage. A malfunction in the availability of loanable funds ripples out to the wider economy, resulting in reduced investment and sales. Production declines and unemployment increases; the economy falls into a recession or even worse, a depression.

During the 1930s, the New Deal Administration of Franklin D. Roosevelt recognized the need to curb risky behavior in the financial markets in order to reduce the vulnerability of the economy. Stringent controls were placed on the behavior of commercial banks, investment banks, brokerages, stock exchanges and the accounting profession. Robert Kuttner writes, "most of the aspects of the market that had gone haywire in the euphoric, laissez-faire 1920s were subjected to regulation."[1]

The Glass-Steagall Act of 1933 was the most important of the new regulatory laws. It restricted commercial banks from engaging in investment bank activities such as selling securities in capital markets, insuring bonds, or acting as

---

[1] Robert Kuttner, *The Squandering of America: How the Failure of Our Politics Undermines Our Prosperity* (New York: Alfred A. Knopf, 2007), p. 10.

brokers in mergers and acquisitions. At the same time, investment banks were barred from most commercial bank activities. Most notably, they were not permitted to offer checking and savings accounts. The commercial banks were provided with deposit insurance, something that was denied to financial houses that engaged in more risky speculative activities. The last piece of this regulatory regime was put in place in 1956, with the passage of the Bank Holding Company Act which prohibited non-bank companies from owning financial houses. In effect, the reward for caution was government insurance and the price for risk was its absence. The entire New Deal regulatory structure was designed to provide secure and stable financing to the real economy. The financial sector was to be a servant, a facilitator for the creation of wealth. And in that objective it was largely successful. Between 1929 and 1985 no major financial crises were experienced in the United States.

Table 6.1

Finance, Insurance and Real Estate Income as Percentage of National Income, Selected Years 1929-2002

Year	Income as Percent of National Income
1929	15.5
1935	12.1
1939	12.4
1950	9.7
1955	10.9
1960	12.0
1965	11.7
1970	11.7
1975	11.5
1980	13.2
1985	14.6
1990	15.9
1995	17.2
2002	20.0

Source: Computed from *Historical Statistics of the United States Earliest Times to the Present*, Millennial Edition, Vol. 3, Table Ca35-53.

But what was a success when seen from one perspective, was a warren's nest of limitations and restrictions that lowered profitability as seen by the firms that made up the financial insurance and real estate sector (FIRE) of the economy. In 1929, as indicated in Table 6.1, and before the imposition of New Deal regulations, FIRE had generated 15.5 percent of the national income. By 1950 that figure was down to 9.7 percent, and as recently as 1975 stood only at 11.5 percent.

Pressured under the regulatory regime, FIRE mounted a political counterattack focused on Congress. It used its wealth to support candidates who would advance its agenda of financial market deregulation. It also engaged in a vast lobbying effort, certain in the knowledge that when its representatives asked for appointments with members of Congress, the memory of contributions and the hope for more ensured that such meetings would take place. Their objective was clear and simple: the dismantling of the financial regulatory system that dated from the New Deal.[2]

No expense was spared. Data compiled by the Center for Responsive Politics (CRP) indicate that since 1990, people associated with FIRE were the single largest source of federal campaign contributions, overall providing in excess of two and a quarter billion dollars to candidates (Table 6.2). Throughout these years, contributions from provided almost one-fifth (19.4 percent) of all political donations (Table 6.3). Only once did FIRE's share of donations dip to as low as 18.1 percent; it reached a high of 21.2 percent in 2000. Though more money was provided to Republican Party candidates, Table 6.3 also makes clear that both major parties were the recipients of FIRE's generous contributions. Democrats were not starved for Wall Street funds. Over these years they received in excess of $1 billion from that source.

---

[2] Ibid., p. 94-105.

Table 6.2
Political Contributions by Sector, 1990-2008

Sector	Amount	Percent to Democrats	Percent to Republicans
Finance, Insurance and Real Estate	2,274,622,193	45	55
Misc Business	1,374,427,851	42	57
Other	1,363,976,942	49	50
Ideology/Single-Issue	1,234,166,197	58	41
Lawyers & Lobbyists	1,204,727,125	70	29
Health	848,358,039	43	56
Labor	673,833,567	92	8
Energy/Nat'l Resources	484,536,679	30	69
Agribusiness	471,052,615	32	68
Construction	453,085,314	33	67
Transportation	400,020,666	33	67
Defense	143,451,528	42	58

Source: Center for Responsive Politics, "Big Picture: Totals by Sector," http://www.opensecrets.org.

Table 6.3
Financial Sector Share of Campaign Financing and Percent Distribution of Financial Sector Political Funding by Party, 1990-2006

Year	Percent of Total	Percent to Democrats	Percent to Republicans
1990	18.6	52	48
1992	19.4	49	50
1994	18.1	49	51
1996	19.5	39	60
1998	19.5	40	60
2000	21.2	41	58
2002	18.6	42	58
2004	19.5	41	58
2006	18.8	44	54
Total	19.4	44	54

Source: See Table 6.2.

FIRE's highest priority was achieved in 1999. Though the Glass-Steagall Act had been weakened by the Federal Reserve under the Chairmanship of Alan Greenspan, the Financial Service Modernization Act repealed it altogether. This broke down the wall between commercial banks and investment banks. The consequence of its doing so was explained by Joseph A. Stiglitz when he wrote that "the most important consequence of the repeal of Glass-Steagall was indirect – it lay in the way repeal changed an entire culture. Commercial banks are not supposed to be high risk ventures; they are supposed to manage other people's money very conservatively.... Investment banks, on the other hand, have traditionally managed rich people's money – people who can take bigger risks in order to get bigger returns. When repeal of Glass-Steagall brought investment and commercial banks together, the investment bank culture came out on top."[3]

A second important triumph for the financial counter-revolution was FIRE's success in resisting the regulation of over-the-counter derivatives. A derivative is a financial instrument whose value is based upon price changes of some other financial asset, such as a contract for the delivery of a commodity at a designated time in the future. The latter - "futures contracts" - are sold on the Chicago Mercantile Exchange and are regulated by the Commodity Futures Trading Commission (CFTC). But contracts based on the movement in prices of other futures contracts - derivatives - are not traded in established markets and therefore are not subject to such supervision. They are sold "over-the-counter."

The risks associated with unregulated derivatives were noticed as early as 1994 in a General Accounting Office (GAO) study. It reported that much of the over-the-counter derivative activity was concentrated among only 15 dealers, many of whom were financially linked to each other. The GAO worried that these linkages would mean that "the sudden failure or abrupt withdrawal from trading of any of these large dealers could cause liquidity problems in the markets and

[3] Joseph A. Stiglitz, "Capitalist Fools," *Vanity Fair*, January 2009, http://www.vanityfair.com/magazine/2009/01/stigltiz200901.

could pose risks to the others, including federally insured banks and the financial system as a whole." A failure by one would mean a failure by others. In an eerie foretelling of what actually was to occur, it warned that if an exogenous shock resulted in the curtailing of trades, the federal government would likely have "to intervene to keep the financial system functioning…."[4]

Picking up on the GAO's warning, Congressman Edward Markey introduced legislation that would have empowered the Securities and Exchange Commission (SEC) to regulate over-the-counter derivatives. But the bill faced opposition not only from FIRE but from the Clinton Administration as well. Undaunted, Brooksley Born, the Chair of the CFTC, argued in support of derivative regulation, concerned that "unfettered opaque trading could threaten our regulated markets or indeed our economy without any federal agency knowing about it."[5] Though Born persevered in her position, her efforts confronted intense industry opposition as well as that from the leading economic figures in government: Alan Greenspan at the Federal Reserve; Lawrence Summers and Robert Rubin, Bill Clinton's most important economic advisors; as well as from members of Congress. Her ultimate defeat was signaled when a provision contained in the Omnibus Spending Bill passed by Congress in 2000, explicitly banned the CFTC from regulating over-the-counter derivatives.

With these two actions – the repeal of Glass Steagall and the prohibition against the regulation of derivatives – Congress completed the counter-revolution that FIRE had sought. Commercial banks were now able to act as investment banks and vice versa, with both able to sell securities and trade in derivatives. As the financial houses eagerly sought new profit opportunities, these unregulated activities grew at the expense of more traditionally staid and conservative bank

---

[4] United States General Accounting Office, *Financial Derivatives: Actions Needed to Protect the Financial System* (Washington D.C.: General Accounting Office, May 1994), p. 7.

[5] Brooksley Born's congressional testimony as quoted in Peter S. Goodman, "Taking Hard New Look at a Greenspan Legacy," *The New York Times*, October 9, 2008, http://www.nytimes.com.

functions. By September 2008 it was estimated that three-quarter of the financial transactions in the United States were barely if at all subject to supervision.[6]

To understand what went wrong in 2007, triggering the most damaging economic downturn since the 1930s Depression, it is important to keep in mind that lending and borrowing is the most important but by no means the most frequently engaged in activity that occurs in the financial sector. Gambling – speculation – is.

When a loan is issued, creditors receive a note, the equivalent of an IOU. Having loaned money in exchange for that IOU, the creditor however is not required to hold onto it until it matures and the loan is repaid. The owner can instead enter a "secondary market" and sell it. Lenders, in this way, can become "liquid." This is to their advantage because they are not required to tie up their capital. If a profitable opportunity arises they can sell the note and obtain cash to use in other investments. But not only is the secondary market advantageous to individual investors. It provides a broader economic function as well. The ability to sell and buy notes in a secondary market means that the level of savings made available is greater than would be the case if such a market did not exist. The liquidity that secondary markets help to create encourages more lending than if the sale of such notes were not possible.

The fact is, however, that participants in the secondary markets are either gamblers themselves - people seeking to profit by correctly anticipating price movements of financial assets (IOU's) - or intermediaries who earn fees promoting such purchases or sales. Since the prices of the IOUs in the secondary markets vary according to their supply and the demand for them, speculators seek to earn income by attempting to correctly anticipating those changes. Predicting an increase in the price of IOUs, they will buy them in order to sell them later and pocket the difference. Alternatively if a speculator expects a fall in the price of IOUs, he or she will sell them now and then buy later at a lower price, again

[6] Charles R. Morris, *The Two Trillion Dollar Meltdown: Easy Money, High Rollers and the Great Credit Crash* (New York: Public Affairs, 2008; Kindle Edition) Location: 2009-15.

keeping the difference. The point is that no matter how sophisticated the techniques used in determining whether to buy or sell, what is basically going on here is bet-making.

Thus there is the ever-present paradox that the existence of secondary markets is necessary for the efficient functioning of the economic system, but that the gamblers and salespeople who participate in them represent a constant threat to the economy's stability. Because secondary markets augment savings and savings pay for investment, those markets contribute to long-term economic growth. But since gamblers are risk-takers who are prone to over-reaching – to underestimating the risks involved in the purchases they make - there is always the possibility that in the absence of close monitoring and regulation, the secondary market will experience a disruption that will damage the economy.

That potential became reality in 2007 with the worst economic downturn since the depression of the 1930s. The problem was that the repeal of Glass-Steagall greatly increased the level of risk that underlay the economy. Prior to the repeal, commercial banks typically originated mortgage loans and maintained ownership of those mortgages until they were paid off in their entirety. But when the wall between commercial banks and investment banks was breached, mortgage issuers sought new and more profitable ways of earning income. One principle activity that they greatly expanded was the packaging and sale of mortgages in products called Collateralized Debt Obligations (CDOs). Instead of holding mortgages until maturity, mortgage issuers sold collections of those loans to other financial institutions, collecting fees for the transactions to replace the interest income they were foregoing. In just four years, between 2001 and 2005, the sale of these packaged mortgages went from $452,000 to $2,274,000.[7]

The problem was that the growth in the market for CDOs was closely associated with a lowering of standards of credit-worthiness for mortgage loans. So long as mortgage lenders earned most of their income from mortgage interest,

---

[7] Yuliya Demyank and Otto Van Hemert, "Understanding the Sub-Prime Mortgage Crisis," *http://wwrm/cp/abstract=1020396*, Table 1.

they had a strong motivation to ensure that borrowers would in fact repay their loans. If financial institutions extended loans to people who were not credit-worthy, and then subsequently those loans became "non-performing," the loan originators took the loss. As a result banks were vigilant in evaluating mortgage applications. To a large extent only credit-worthy applicants obtained mortgages.

All of that changed with the explosive growth in the use of CDOs. Now the original lender was likely to sell the mortgage as part of a package long before the loan matured. Crucially, since the lenders did not intend to hold the mortgages until the loan's maturity, banks and other mortgage providers became less assiduous in scrutinizing the credit-worthiness of potential loan recipients. Because they expected to sell the mortgages, they were less concerned about the repayment of these loans. A default would be someone else's problem. Thus emerged the growing importance of "sub-prime mortgages," loans extended to home buyers who in the past would not have been deemed credit-worthy.

The increased risks associated with this changed behavior by financial institutions were masked for a time by two other developments. The first was that the CDOs typically were evaluated by rating agencies paid by the CDO sellers themselves. That meant that a conflict of interest was deeply embedded in the process. On one side, rating agencies are private firms looking to secure income by contracting to do risk evaluations. On the other side, CDO holders are seeking the highest possible credit rating in order to maximize the price at which they could sell the package of mortgages. Since the rating agencies were paid by the CDO sellers, they were under pressure to rubber stamp high ratings as a means to secure their own income stream and profitability. If a rating agency failed to provide a high score, the CDO holders could simply take their business elsewhere. The upshot was a dramatic over-valuation of the credit-worthiness of CDOs. This induced financial institutions to make purchases that they otherwise might not have, purchases that in their turn encouraged the issuing of even more mortgages and sales of CDOs.

The second way in which the growing fragility of the financial system was masked is traceable to the housing price inflation – the bubble – that occurred in these years. In inflation-adjusted prices the median price of houses in the United States increased from under $150,000 in 1998 to almost $270,000 just eight years later in 2006.[8] Since this bubble provided mortgage holders with additional equity in their homes, borrowers who fell behind on their housing loans were able to use their now more valuable property to secure a second mortgage and pay off the first. Refinancing became the norm, shielding both borrowers and lenders from the damage that would occur from defaults. With this came yet another self-reinforcing mechanism. The failure to take risk sufficiently into account in issuing the loan in the first place, occasioned by the advent of CDOs, meant the risk of default was high, thereby increasing the likelihood that a second mortgage would be needed.

But when the upward movement in housing prices halted, all of this unraveled rapidly. With the end of housing price inflation, the resulting reduction in collateral meant that refinancing became more difficult and for many people simply impossible. Defaults thereby increased. Thus when the bubble burst, financial institutions were confronted with a serious loss of income. The revenue that they anticipated receiving from the packages of mortgages they owned went into a sharp decline. With that the case, those institutions experienced a fall-off in their own ability to extend new loans. Further, because they owned a growing number of non-performing loans they themselves were confronted with the threat – and in many cases the reality - of insolvency. And finally, banks became fearful about extending loans to other financial institutions, worried that those banks - as holders of mortgages - were under pressure and would be unable to repay. The consequence was that credit all but dried up. As a result, household consumption and business investment, denied the credit needed to make purchases, went into a tailspin.

---

[8] "United States House Prices," http://mysite.verizon.net/vzeqrguz/housingbubble.

This combination of events is a clear case of the tail wagging the dog. Instead of providing a mechanism to channel savings reliably into productive investment, financial markets were allowed to become oversized and out of control, ultimately bringing down the real economy of production, consumption, and employment. Increasingly able to escape regulation and venture into profitable but risky activities, symbolized by but not confined to the CDO market, FIRE became increasingly profitable and as a result became an ever larger sector of the economy. As shown in Table 6.1, between 1950 and 2002 that share increased from 9.7 percent to 20.0, an all time high. But, of course, the country came to pay a high price for FIRE' explosive growth. When FIRE fell apart because it was built on a foundation of highly risky ventures, it brought the entire economy down with it.

This catastrophe occurred in large part because FIRE was able to leverage its wealth politically. No sector of the economy could match its role as political campaign financier, and no sector received more in return for its investment. This occurred because in a privately financed political system a wealthy faction, to employ Madison's formulation, like FIRE can come to play a disproportionate role in influencing policy. With that, factional interests trump society's interests. But the mere fact that the role played by FIRE in the economic crisis is widely understood by no means ensures that political corrective action will be undertaken. FIRE retains its political clout and can be expected to fight any efforts to reduce its ability to engage in profitable but risky activity.[9]

One way that Wall Street's size could be reduced in order to make it better serve the economy would be by imposing a tax on financial transactions, a tax known as a security taxation excise tax (STET). This is a sales tax that would be imposed on all transactions involving stocks, bonds and other financial products such as CDO's. Such a tax would do two things simultaneously. It would make

---

[9] See, for example, Alison Vikskin and Dawn Kopecki, "Not So Radical Reform: How New Democrats and Wall Street are Watering down Financial Regulation in Congress," *BusinessWeek*, January 11, 2010, pp. 24-29.

trading in risky financial assets less profitable, and it would generate a lot of revenue for the Treasury - both desirable outcomes.

Of course imposing a STET is not the only way to reshape FIRE. Certainly there is ample justification for curbing its most speculative projects. For this, enhanced market regulations are needed. But despite the availability of such other options, it remains the case that nothing is quite so effective as a tax. Regulatory agencies unfortunately are routinely captured by those whom they are intended to regulate. But if the legislation is carefully drawn there is no way to defang a tax. Making financial speculation less profitable would redirect resources away from the form of legalized gambling that still prevails in the financial sector, with the likelihood that productive activities will benefit.

No one really knows how much revenue a STET would raise. But whatever its level, it could not begin to compensate the people of the country for the damage that FIRE has imposed on them. Its value rather would be in the anticipation that if it reduces Wall Street's importance in the economy, calamities such as the recent economic crisis would not recur.

As attractive as a STET seems, it would take a political donnybrook to pass the legislation necessary to implement it. Just how difficult it would be is suggested by FIRE's contribution to the Congressional committees that would be responsible for its drafting. In 2007 and 2008 members of the House Financial Services Committee and the Senate Banking, Housing and Urban Affairs Committee received $25.2 million and $40.2 million respectively from individuals and PACs associated with FIRE. These sums are more than twice the level that members of these committees received from any other single sector of the economy. FIRE's contributions to the House committee members came to 27.0 percent of the total campaign funds they raised. The comparable percentage for members of the Senate committee was 29.4 percent.[10] Obviously these

[10] Computed from Center for Responsive Politics, "House Financial Services Committee, 111th Congress (2008 cycle): Overview" and "Senate Banking, Housing and Urban Affairs Committee, 111th Congress (2008 cycle); "Overview," http://www.opensecrets.org.

disproportionately large donations to strategically placed members of Congress are intended to influence the legislation emerging from these two committees. It is certain that a STET is not a project that is endorsed by these contributors.

But the resentment of Wall Street in the country runs deep. The very banks that caused the economic crisis have been the beneficiaries of government handouts. Further, the pain that has been experienced extends widely over the whole society. This resentment however is not well focused, and in any case popular anger cannot begin to compete with FIRE on the terrain upon which the latter is strongest: providing campaign funds to politicians.

Madison was right. Public policy should never predominantly be responsive to a self-selected faction. There is too great a danger that society's interests will be sacrificed for those of the special interest group. Yet it is precisely that danger that will be present as long as our political system depends upon private funding. Most people cannot afford to make the big political donations that politicians require. As a result, office-seekers are more responsive to large donors than to their non-contributing constituents.

The economic crisis represents only a specific instance of a more general problem. Because it is so rich, the financial community exercises a great deal of political influence. But precisely because FIRE is so important to the economy, that political influence can be very costly to the society as a whole. The goal of public policy therefore should be to curtail the financial sector's political clout in order to have it function efficiently in the service of the entire economy. To do that FIRE's ability to use its wealth to advance its short-term interests must be offset.

That can be accomplished by placing everyone in the electoral arena on an equal footing. Special interests in politics cannot be eliminated. But a rough equality of special interest influence can be achieved. What we need to do is get closer to the objective that Madison sought: a politics in which factions are denied disproportionate influence.

Chapter 7
The Crisis of Health Care

The protracted 2009 debate about medical care in the United States occurred because too many people lacked health insurance, health care was too costly, and in important ways the health of the American people was inferior to citizens of other countries at comparable levels of economic development. The debate was fruitful because it seems likely that, as of this writing that something close to universal health insurance will be enacted. It is likely furthermore that the extension of health insurance to those who previously were uninsured will have a positive effect on health outcomes. It will allow for more and earlier treatment and thereby almost certainly will result in improved medical outcomes. At the same time however other, important weaknesses in the country's health care system seem likely to go unattended. In particular significant inroads will not be made in lowering the costs of health services. In the legislation that likely to be adopted, little attention is devoted to curbing the prices of medicines. The same is true with regard to the fee for service system. That system presently creates an upward bias to costs because it rewards health care providers each time a procedure is performed. These omissions represent missed opportunities not only to curb the rise in costs, but as well to advance well-being. Lower pharmaceutical prices would enable more people to gain access to medicines. And reducing the scope of the fee for service system could well result in the medical industry's offering more preventive care than it does at present. With that, there would be a diminution in the present perverse system in which practitioners are paid only if the people they administer to become ill.

Among comparable nations only the United States fails to guarantee medical care to anyone who gets sick.[1] Even so, health care as a share of the gross domestic product is greater here than in any of the other countries under consideration. In the United States, 15.3 percent of the country's 2005 gross domestic product was spent on health care compared to the mean of 9.2 percent for the fourteen other countries listed in Table 7.1. No nation in that list comes close to the United States with respect to the cost of health care relative to other sectors of its economy. Despite this, the United States ranks next to last in female life expectancy at birth and last in male life expectancy at birth.

Table 7.1

Life Expectancy at Birth by Gender and Health Expenditures as Percent GDP for Selected Countries, 2005

	Female	Male	As % GDP
United States	**80.4**	**75.2**	**15.3**
Australia	83.3	78.5	9.5
Austria	82.2	76.7	10.2
Belgium	81.6	75.8	10.3
Denmark	80.2	75.6	9.1
France	83.8	76.7	11.1
Germany	81.8	76.2	10.7
Italy	83.2	77.6	8.9
Japan	85.5	78.6	8.0
Netherlands	81.6	77.2	9.2
Norway	82.5	77.7	9.1
Spain	83.9	77.4	8.2
Sweden	82.8	78.4	9.1
Switzerland	83.9	78.7	11.6
United Kingdom	81.1	76.9	8.2
Mean Excluding United States	**82.7**	**77.1**	**9.2**

Source: U.S. Census Bureau, *Statistical Abstract of the United States, 2009* (Washington DC, 2008), Tables 1296 and 1301.

[1] T. R. Reid, *The Healing of America: A Global Quest for Better, Cheaper and Fairer Health Care* (New York: The Penguin Press, 2009), p. 3

In light of all of this it is not surprising that reforming the American health care system was a major plank in Barack Obama's presidential campaign platform and has been a priority for his administration from its inception. In his speech to a joint session of Congress on September 9, 2009, the President called attention to the fact that nearly a century earlier Theodore Roosevelt had called for health care reform and that "ever since, nearly every President and Congress, whether Democrat or Republican has attempted to meet this challenge in some way." Obama declared that "our collective failure to meet this challenge – year after year, decade after decade – has led us to the breaking point."[2]

The predominant form by which Americans gain access to health care is by securing employment-based health insurance - insurance policies partially paid for by employers. Almost 60 percent of the American people obtain their health care in this way. Another roughly 30 percent possess a government health insurance policy such as Medicaid or Medicare. About three-eighths of these people possess both private and public insurance. That leaves a significant percentage of Americans without any health insurance at all.[3]

This pattern is unique to the United States. Among all comparably industrialized nations health insurance is universal, recognized as a right to which everyone is entitled. As T.R. Reid puts it, "all the developed countries…provide health coverage for every resident, old or young, rich or poor," except the United States. Typically this health insurance is offered either by the state or by tightly regulated companies that are not permitted to seek a maximum return on their investment. The United States is an exception in this regard because, as Reid puts it "… it relies so heavily on for-profit private insurance plans to pay the bills."[4]

---

[2] The White House, Office of the Press Secretary, "Remarks by the President to a Joint Session of Congress on Health Care," http://www.whitehouse.gov.

[3] DeNavas-Walt, Carmen, Bernadette D. Proctor and Jessica C. Smith, U.S. Census Bureau, Current Population Reports, P60-236, Income , *Poverty and Health Insurance Coverage in the United States, 2008* (Washington DC: U.S. Government Printing Office, 2009), Table C-1.

[4] T.R. Reid, *The Healing of America: A Global Quest for Better, Cheaper and Fairer Health Care* p. 21, 23. The following paragraph is based on this work, pp. 17-19.

There are three different models by which health care is delivered, each of which contrasts with the market-based system in this country. In Germany, Japan, France, Belgium, and Switzerland medical costs are tightly regulated by the government. In these nations health providers are private, compensated by non-profit health insurance plans that are financed by employers and employees. In this model, medical costs are tightly regulated by the government. A second approach is the one employed in Great Britain, Spain, and most of the Scandinavian countries. With it, health care is both provided and financed by the government, paid for with tax revenues. Hospitals and clinics are publicly owned and most physicians are public sector employers. There are doctors in private practice, but they too collect their fees from the government. In this approach, costs are maintained at low levels since the government, as the sole payer, controls doctors' compensation. And third, there is the method used in Canada combining features of both of the above. In it, health care is provided by private doctors and hospitals, but a government-run insurance program is the single source of compensation. Here too costs are maintained at low levels because there are no insurance marketing costs and the single payer uses its market power to negotiate low drug prices.

In all health care systems, insurance plays a strategic role. It governs who has access to medical attention and how much and what kind of medical care is to be provided. But in this area too the United States differs markedly from other countries. As Reid explains, "foreign health insurance plans exist only to pay people's medical bills, not to make a profit. The United States is the only nation that lets insurance companies extract a profit from basic health coverage." Put another way, again quoting Reid, the "basic building block in the health care systems of every wealthy country – except the United States – is the principle that financing health care must be a non-profit endeavor."[5]

---

[5] ibid, p. 236, 235.

The health care models employed in other countries could have provided a template for the reform of the American health care system. President Obama was aware of these alternatives. He acknowledged that there are those, as he put it, "on the left who believe that the only way to fix the system is through a single-payer system like Canada's…where we would severely restrict the private insurance market and have the government provide coverage for everybody." However, at the same time, he also cited an approach favored by the political right in this country, even though this model is not practiced anywhere in the developed world. In it, health insurance is purchased individually on a voluntary basis – without the employer-based insurance system. Ultimately, the President rejected both. Eschewing "a radical shift that would disrupt the health care most people currently have," he maintained that "it makes more sense to build on what works and fix what doesn't, rather than try to build an entirely new system from scratch."[6]

In adopting this incrementalist approach to reform, President Obama no doubt was aware of the long history of attempted and failed efforts at health care reform in this country that preceded his presidency. Dating back to the New Deal and Franklin D. Roosevelt's inability to merge universal health insurance with social security, this issue has been a nightmare for public policy. Harry S. Truman tried but was unable to establish national health insurance, and neither could Bill Clinton succeed in instituting a system of managed health care. The only exception was Lyndon B. Johnson's success in the 1960s in securing insurance for the elderly and poor with Medicare and Medicaid. It was this pattern of disappointment that the Obama Administration was obviously determined to avoid.[7]

---

[6] "Remarks by the President to a Joint Session of Congress on Health Care." http:www.whitehouse.gov/the-press-office/remarks-by-the-president-to-a-joint-session-of-congress-on-health-care.

[7] David Blumenthal and James A. Morone, *The Heart of Power: Health and Politics in the Oval Office* (Berkeley, Los Angeles, London: University of California Press, 2009) pp. 21-98, 346-384.

The Obama strategy not only rejected using other countries' health care systems as a model, adopting instead a piecemeal strategy of change, but as well he chose to prioritize the expansion of health insurance coverage as compared to the problem of the high costs of the American system. Most of what was presented for example on the White House website was concerned with improving the availability of health care insurance for people who already possessed coverage or with making it easier for the uninsured to be covered. The list of proposals included requiring large employers to provide insurance coverage (or else pay a fee), ending discrimination against people with pre-existing conditions, limiting premium discrimination based on gender and age, preventing insurance companies from dropping coverage when people are sick, capping out-of-pocket medical expenses, eliminating charges for preventive care and prescription drug expenditures, and creating an insurance market ("exchanges") for people without coverage.[8]

In contrast, the President had little to say with regard to the problem of costs. He did suggest providing incentives for hospitals to prevent avoidable readmissions and giving support for new models of care delivered through medical homes. Further the President proposed that an independent commission of doctors and medical experts be created "to make recommendations to Congress each year on how to promote greater efficiency and higher quality in Medicare." Finally, the President hopes to reform medical malpractice law, though specifically he recommended only that the Secretary of Health and Human Services "...move forward on awarding medical malpractice demonstration grants to states...."[9] These suggestions, however were little more than window-dressing. Even in combination they are inadequate to the task of curbing costs.

Obama's suggestions fail to seriously engage the problem of costs at each level of the United State medical system - the incomes of health professionals, the

---

[8] "The Obama Plan: Stability and Security for all Americans," http://www.whitehouse.gov/issues/health_care/plan.
[9] The White House, "Remarks by the President to a Joint Session of Congress on Health Care."

costs of hospital care and testing procedures, and the pricing of medicines and health insurance premiums. All are part of the production chain and each bears at least partial responsibility for the high health care costs experienced in this country. A serious cost containment project would have to address the role played by each. It would have to offer mechanisms that either reduce the income received by one or more of them or that introduce efficiencies to significantly lower costs.

However, there was one proposal put forward by the White House that did hold out a promise of reducing costs, though by late September 2009 it had been removed from its website. This would have offered a public health insurance option. Such an innovation would represent a cost-containment strategy to the extent that the government insurance company offered lower cost coverage than the private firms and thereby represented a substantial competitive threat to them. Even in offering this alternative however, the President went out of his way to insist in his health care address to the Congress that its applicability would be severely restricted. The President's estimate was that less than five percent of Americans would sign up, thereby marginalizing its impact. Even so, as President Obama himself acknowledged, the insurance companies did not like this idea, and he seemed to back away from it with the remark that it was only a means to an end "and we should remain open to other ideas that accomplish our ultimate goal.[10]

Extending health insurance to the uninsured is expensive. Subsidies in one form or another – either to insurance companies or to the uninsured – are necessary in order to increase the coverage rate from the level achieved without financial incentives. But President Obama vowed that extending coverage should not be allowed to increase the federal government's budget deficit. Thus, the extent to which the necessary incentives can be provided and full insurance coverage can be achieved is dependent upon the government's ability to raise the necessary funds. The President argued that "reducing the waste and inefficiency

---

[10] The White House, "Remarks by the President to a Joint Session of Congress on Health Care."

in Medicare and Medicaid will pay for most of this plan," and that an increase in taxes on pharmaceutical firms and insurance companies would make up any short-fall.[11] But it remains to be seen whether these two sources of funding will be adequate, especially if the objective is universal health insurance coverage. If not, it will be necessary to scale back the efforts to enroll all previously uninsured individuals.

The order of magnitude of the sums involved in health care reform was made clear by the Congressional Budget Office (CBO) when it examined the costs of one of the major proposals considered in the House of Representatives, H.R. 3200, "America's Affordable Health Choices Act." This bill was reasonably faithful to the President's objectives. If passed, it would establish a health insurance mandate, expand eligibility for Medicaid, create health insurance exchanges, and provide tax credits to small employers who contribute toward the cost of health insurance. Collectively these provisions, the CBO reported, would reduce the number of uninsured individuals by about 37 million at a cost of slightly more that $1 trillion over a ten year period.[12] A subsequent bill authored by Senate Finance Committee Chairman Max Baucus, similar in content but somewhat scaled down, would cost $856 billion over the same ten years and extend coverage to even fewer uninsured Americans.[13]

Despite the difficulties, the Obama Administration in fact is likely to achieve an expansion of health insurance coverage. Universal health insurance probably will not be secured, but the advances that will be achieved are important and welcome. But because this will be accomplished without addressing and containing the level at which medical professionals, hospitals, insurance companies and pharmaceutical firms are compensated, there is a very real risk

---

[11] Ibid.

[12] U.S. Congressional Budget Office, Douglas W. Elmendorf, Director, "Letter to Honorable Charles B. Rangel, Chairman, Committee on Ways and Means, U.S. House of Representatives, July 17, 2009.

[13] Reuters, "Factbox: Details of Baucus Plan for U.S. Healthcare Reform," September 17, 2009, *http://www.reuters.com/articlePrinct?articleID=US* TRE58G3250090917.

that the problem of rising medical costs will intensify. With the Obama reforms, access to medical services will increase without a corresponding reduction in the costs associated with the supply of those services. Demand will grow more than will supply. With that, both the prices paid for health care either as payments made out of pocket, or as insurance premiums, or by Medicare/Medicaid payments can go only one way – up. Notwithstanding the gains that will be secured by people who previously were uninsured, this looks very much like a bonanza for the health care industry, particularly insurance companies and pharmaceutical firms.

There is no doubt that Barack Obama knows that modernizing the United States health care system requires not only that medical services have to be made available to everyone but also that the cost of those services has to be contained. Nevertheless he pursued only a partial solution to the problem of health care in this country, largely avoiding the cost side. It seems likely that the President's judgment was that the opponents of comprehensive reform were simply too powerful to be taken on. As hard as it is to extend insurance coverage, it would have been much more difficult to pass legislation to reduce the incomes of one or more of the providers of medical care and treatment. Instead President Obama opted to attempt to secure incremental insurance coverage gains without engaging in a frontal battle over costs. Reducing health care costs was left for another day.

The industries and professions that play a role in providing medical treatment to the American people by and large are the recipients of above-average income flows. Physicians and dentists ranked number one and number two among all occupations in median earnings according to the census of 2000 (the latest year for which data are available).[14] Further, according to *Fortune* magazine, firms producing medical products and equipment ranked 10th, pharmaceuticals 12th and health insurance 17th among the top 51 industries, each with a return on

---

[14] U.S. Census Bureau "Evidence from Census 2000 about Earnings by Detailed Occupation for Men and Women," (Issued May 2004),Figure 3. http://www.census.gov/prod/2004pubs/censr-15.pdf.

shareholders' equity of 19.0 percent or more, far higher than the median for the top industries of 15.0 percent.[15] As such, the members of this sector possess the financial resources that allow them to work effectively in the political realm to protect their privileged status. It is of course true that the interests of these firms and individuals are not in every case identical. Insurance companies would like to see the fees paid to physicians minimized, while doctors and surgeons would like to have payments for services as high as possible. Despite their conflicts however, all are participants in the same industry and share an interest in maintaining it as a high income-generating sector.

To that end the health care sector has been an important source of campaign funding for politicians. Through its contributions it hopes to construct a self-reinforcing cycle of prosperity. As donors they gain access to and can effectively persuade office-holders to respond favorably to their interests. To the degree that they are successful in this regard, they can ensure their continued status as high income earners.

Table 7.2

Political Contributions of Health Care and Insurance Sectors, 2008 ($ millions)

Sector	*Sub-sector*	*Amount*
Health		**166.6**
	Health Professionals	95.2
	Hospitals/Nursing Homes	23.3
	Health Services/HMOs	14.3
	Pharmaceuticals	29.2
	Other	4.6
Insurance		**46.8**

Source: Center for Responsive Politics, "Totals by Sector," http://www.opensecrets.org.

---

15 Fortune 500, Top Industries: Most Profitable, Return on Shareholders' Equity. Measured by return on assets, Medical Products and Equipment ranked #2, Pharmaceuticals #6, and Health Care Insurance #16. *http://money.cnn.com/magazines/fortune/fortune* 500/2008.

According to the Center for Responsive Politics (CRP), in the 2008 election year cycle alone the health sector contributed $166.6 million to Congressional candidates, ranking it fifth among all sectors in contributions (Table 7.2). "Health professionals," presumably mostly physicians, contributed more than half (57.1 percent) of these funds. It is important to note furthermore that the estimate of the health sector campaign donations is an underestimate. Not included are donations made by people associated with the health insurance industry. This exclusion occurs because in the CRP data, insurance is included in the finance, insurance and real estate (FIRE) sector. No information is provided on the question of how much of FIRE's contributions come from health insurers in contrast for example to home owners or automobile insurance companies. The best that be said is that not only is $166.6 million a great deal of money, but it is certain that even more than that amount was donated by people interested in blocking health care reform.

Just as it would be difficult to imagine that expenditures of this magnitude would have no effect on the politics of health care reform, it is equally unlikely that donors would continue to make cash contributions in these amounts unless they believed they were having the desired result. But as if to make certain that their message was being heard, the health sector spent almost a half billion additional dollars in 2008 ($484.4 million) on lobbying.[16] In 2009 the pace picked up even more with the CRP reporting that in the second quarter of 2009 alone, the health sector spent more than $133 million on lobbying. No sector spent more on lobbying in this period.[17]

By August 2009, it was clear that these efforts had borne fruit. In its August 6, 2009 issue, *BusinessWeek* carried a story entitled "The Health Insurers Have Already Won," and on August 24, 2009 an article appeared in *The Los Angeles Times* with the headline "Healthcare Insurers Get Upper Hand," with a

---

[16] Center for Responsive Politics, "Diagnosis: Reform," http:www.opensecrets.org.

[17] Center for Responsive Politics, Capital Eye Blog, "Health, Energy and Finance Sectors Dominate 2nd Quarter Lobbying," http://www.opensecrets.org.

sub-title that was even more graphic: "Obama's Overhaul Fight is Being Won by the Industry, Experts Say. The End Result May Be a Financial 'Bonanza.'" These articles detailed how the health insurance industry, worried about the public option idea that had been mooted by the President and liberal members of Congress, had lobbied strongly against it. Though liberals like House Speaker Nancy Pelosi continued to support the public option at that stage in the debate, the *BusinessWeek* article reported "the [health insurance] industry has already accomplished its main goal of at least curbing and maybe blocking altogether any new publicly-administered insurance program that could grab market share from the corporations that dominate the business." This reading of Congressional sentiment was confirmed several weeks later when in mid-September Senator Baucus went public with his health care reform plan and revealed that it did not contain a public option. Further, this same report goes on to say that the industry "also achieved a secondary aim of constraining the new benefits that will become available to tens of millions of people who are currently uninsured."[18]

The role of the government in providing medical coverage had all along been the biggest source of anxiety, not only for the insurance companies, but for other members of the health care industry as well. The concern was that a public sector insurance provider would have the ability to reduce revenue flows. If enough people enrolled in the public option, the government could strongly influence medical fees, insurance premiums, drug costs, and hospital finances. And indeed proposals for an even bigger role for government than a public option were being made, usually packaged as extending "medicare for all." This was the message for example of an article written by George S. McGovern in *The*

[18] Chad Terhune and Keith Epstein, "The Health Insurers Have Already Won," *BusinessWeek*, August 6, 2009. *http://www.businessweek.com/print/magazine/content/09_33/b4143034820260.htm*; Tom Hamburger and Kim Geiger, "Health Insurers Get Upper Hand," *Los Angeles Times*, August 24, 2009, *http://www/latimes.com/news/nationworld/washingtondc/la-na-healthcare-insurers24-2009aug24,0,4551786.story*. The Baucus plan did however include a provision for the start up of non-profit cooperatives that would compete with private insurers. Reuters, Fact box, "Details of Baucus Plan for U.S. Healthcare Reform."

Washington Post, where he charged that the role played by health insurance companies was "a major reason Americans pay more for health care per capita than any other people in the world."[19] But though enhancing the role of the government would be a potentially effective strategy to accomplish what otherwise is an all but impossible task – increasing health coverage and at the same time controlling costs – this was precisely the nightmare scenario the industry set out to quash. In this, its lobbyists and publicists were quite aggressive, including in their repertoire the use of the epithet that what was being proposed was "socialized medicine." In the end, the health care sector, with the insurance companies in the lead, prevailed. "Medicare for all" was not seriously considered in the Congress nor was the public option anywhere to be seen as the legislative process churned to its conclusion.[20]

The internal politics among the groups within the health care sector are complex; unanimity on all issues does not prevail. Though the pharmaceutical firms teamed up with the insurance companies and the American Medical Association (AMA) in opposition to a public insurance option,[21] in fact a majority of practicing physicians do not share this resistance to reform. A recent survey of physicians reported in *The New England Journal of Medicine* reported that 62.9 percent believed that both a public health insurance option as well as private insurance plans should be made available. Breaking ranks even more, 58% percent of physicians supported an expansion of Medicare to Americans between the ages of 55 and 64.[22]

Similar disagreements exist within the population generally. Survey data reveal that the emotional opposition expressed in a number of 2009 town hall

---

[19] George S. McGovern, "It's Simple: Medicare for All," *The Washington Post*, September 13, 2009, http://www.washingtonpost.com.

[20] Katharine Q. Seelye, "Medicare for All? 'Crazy,' 'Socialized' and Unlikely," *The New York Times*, September 19, 2009, http://prescriptions.blogs.nytimes.com.

[21] Robert Reich, "How Pharma and Insurance intend to Kill the Public Option, And What Obama and the Rest of Us Must Do, *Wall Street Pit*, June 6, 2009, http://www.wallstreetpit.com.

[22] Salomeh Keyhani and Alex Federman, "Doctors on Coverage – Physicians' Views on a New Public Insurance Option and Medicare Expansion, *The New England Journal of Medicine*, September 14, 2009, www.nejm.org.

meetings to the Obama health reform represents a substantial, but by no means majority, point of view. On the contrary, polls reveal majority support for reforms that are more extensive than those proposed by the Obama administration. A Kaiser Family Foundation Health Poll in July 2009 for example reported that 77 percent of respondents supported expanding Medicare to cover people between 55 and 64, 58 percent agreed that Medicare should expand to cover everyone, and 50 percent supported a single payer system.[23] In corroboration, a survey carried out for Bloomberg News at the same time indicated that 61 percent of those asked thought that it was "critically important" to "find a way for those who are currently uninsured to get health insurance coverage." In addition, 54 percent thought it "critically important" to "hold down the costs individuals currently pay for premiums, deductibles and co-pays." The Bloomberg poll did not inquire about attitudes toward a public option or a government-run program, though it did reveal that 52 percent believed that the claim that health care reform would lead to "socialized medicine" was a "distortion/scare tactic," compared to the 43 percent who though the argument was "legitimate."[24] Thus though the opposition to an enhanced role for the government is intense, it is far from a majority viewpoint.

Indeed these data suggest that the public's view on the issue of health care has been marginalized in the Congress, articulated only by a few liberals whose submissions are not being seriously considered. This is not to say that this popular support would be sustained if the expansion of Medicare or adoption of a single payer system were to be taken up in earnest in the Congress. In debate, flaws might well be identified and if so support would erode. But the point is that the process does not get that far. The majority point of view was not even being debated.

In this way the politics of health care resembles that of climate change and the financial crisis. All three reveal the disproportionate influence of private

[23] The Henry J. Kaiser Family Foundation, *Kaiser Health Tracking Poll (July 7-14, 2009)*, Publication #7943, www.kff.org.

[24] *Bloomberg Poll on Obama, Health Care, Economy: Results Chart*, September 16, 2009, http://www.bloomberg.com/apps/news?pid=20601070&sid=a1aj4z4GhbH8.

donors in the political process. In the case of the financial system, political funders used their clout to secure deregulation, while the energy and health care vested interests were successful in impeding popular reforms that had the potential to be effective. What fundamentally unites all three cases is the fact that the money that donors provide to politicians drives a deep wedge between the public's preferences and the policies that office holders promote and enact.

Chapter 8

Creating a Social Movement

Campaign finance reform has never generated a social movement. As the researchers at the Center for Responsive Politics (CRP) have noted, "the historic social movements that have been responsible for the evolution of American democracy focused primarily on electoral participation – especially voting rights broadly defined – and scarcely at all on electoral finance." Citing the victories secured by women and African Americans with regard to the right to vote, the CRP argues that "these struggles can be seen as efforts to nullify or at least counterbalance the undemocratic influence of the monied elites on the political process." Nevertheless, they write, neither "directly challenged the primary institution by which the monied elites exercised political control – privately financed election campaigns."[1] Indeed, in his definitive study of the the right to vote in the United States, Alexander Keyssar mentions the subject only once and then only to bemoan the fact that "the raw and growing power of money in politics serves as a counterweight to the democratic thrust of the twentieth-century broadening of suffrage" and that "the current state of American politics

---

[1] Center for Responsive Politics, "A Brief History of Money in Politics: Campaign Finance and Campaign Finance Reform in the United States." This document no longer is available at the Center's website, but it has been reproduced in part by the Hoover Institution at http://www.campaignfinancesite.org/history/reform1.html.

makes clear that universal suffrage is a necessary but not sufficient condition for a fully democratic political order."[2]

With this said, and without denying the dominant role private wealth continues to play in the contemporary political system, the fact remains that the period since the early 1970s has seen more activity and legislation with regard to campaign financing than at any other time in United States history. Private wealth in politics has not been tamed. But significant legislation has been passed: at the national level the Federal Election Campaign Act (FECA) limited campaign contributions, required that substantial political contributions be made public, and provided for the public financing of presidential candidates. A dozen years later the Bipartisan Campaign Reform Act (BCRA) was legislated, banning "soft money" contributions. A handful of states and municipalities adopted systems that provide a publicly funded option for candidates running for office. In most cases, once adopted these public funded systems have been sustained; robust efforts by opponents to have them scuttled have failed. In short, despite the fact that the social movements that have deepened democracy have not placed a high priority on campaign finance reform, the issue today exists as a presence on the political agenda.

At one level it is easy to explain why movements to extend the suffrage to women and African Americans did not include the role of private wealth in politics. It was difficult enough to secure the right to vote – a basic component of citizenship. To complicate that struggle with a different though related concern would likely have compromised whatever chances existed for success. Both movements required that allies be secured outside of their ranks, but the probabilities of their doing so would have declined if they had extended their demands beyond the right to vote.

It might also be argued that campaign finance reform is at a disadvantage compared to other issues in fueling a mass movement because it is a process

---

[2] Alexander Keyssar, *The Right to Vote: The Contested History of Democracy in the United States* (New York: Basic Books, 2000), p. 322.

issue, unable to promise specific outcomes. It is concerned that electoral campaigns are carried out fairly, but does not endorse specific programs and policies that might emerge from a more fair political process. Aside from achieving a greater degree of equality in the political system, it is not possible for its advocates to guarantee that specific reforms or social advances will be achieved if the role of private wealth in politics is reduced.

The fact is however that the historical struggle for the vote was also focused on a process issue. With increased access to the ballot box, all that could be said with confidence was that the ranks of the electorate would be swelled as the previously excluded population took advantage of the opportunity to vote. Aside from the likelihood that the political process would generally become more responsive to the interests of those newly voting constituents, nothing more concrete could be promised. Despite this, a mass movement in support of the right to vote became powerful enough to end decades of discrimination against women and African American voters.

Those movements benefited from the strongly held consensus view that the right to vote is fundamental to American society. As Keyssar writes, the "democratic self-image" in the United States is that "the right to vote is and long has been widely distributed among Americans, that the United States has something very close to universal suffrage." As he writes, "in popular usage the term democracy implies that everyone or nearly everyone has the right to participate in elections." With this the case, advocates for the disenfranchised were able to align their political objectives with the basic contours of American political culture. Thus, in 1957 the Commission on Civil Rights argued that the South, in denying African Americans the right to vote, revealed "a striking gap between our principles and our everyday practices. This is a moral gap.....It runs counter to our traditional concepts of fair play. It is a partial repudiation of our faith in the democratic system."[3]

---

[3] Alexander Keyssar, *The Right to Vote*, p. xvi, 260.

No such supportive consensus prevails concerning the need to curtail the role of private wealth in the political process. Whereas those who would deny the right to vote could be considered un-American, that charge often is directed against activists who seek greater equality in the funding of election campaigns. To be sure, the argument that private wealth in politics distorts the process and violates the American commitment to political equality can be made. But the point is that it is an argument that does not draw the nearly unanimous assent that is present when, for example, the claim is made that no one should be denied the right to vote.

The commonsense understanding of democracy in the United States thus embodies an internal contradiction. The right to vote is affirmed and all citizens are considered politically equal. But no comparably strong agreement exists that denies the legitimacy of wealth in dominating election results. According to John Dunn, American democracy despite its formal political equality is "aristocratic in substance." It rests on the use of the market economy, described by him as "the most powerful mechanism for dismantling equality that humans have ever forged."[4]

Dunn provides important insights into the mechanisms in the United States that have militated against equality's becoming more than simply the right to vote. He argues that the appeal of economic equality has been blunted because of "the unpromising instruments for realizing it and the rigidities inherent in its pursuit." By this Dunn seems to be pointing both to the brutal revolutions that brought communists to power and to the repellent and undemocratic nature of the regimes they created. Referring to communism as "equality on stilts," Dunn writes that "the route to equality has always proved savagely divisive," and as a result "requires of any ruler who tries to implement it extreme and permanent

---

[4] John Dunn, *Setting the People Free: The Story of Democracy* (London: Atlantic Books, 2005, pp. 174, 124, 125, 137.

coercion…."[5] The cause of equality thus has been grievously damaged by the political behavior of those acting in its name.

In addition Dunn argues that in the United States, advocates of equality have been hurt by the political use of wealth by their adversaries: "on the terrain where they [the proponents of equality] must secure their victory in the end, in elections to Congress and to the presidency, they were always to find themselves heavily out-spent and out-voted." The political system was rigged, with the wealthy able to use their resources to both ensure legislation favorable to their interests and to place roadblocks in the path of egalitarian efforts.[6]

But Dunn's counter-posing markets and democracy as inherently contradictory is overstated. Indeed egalitarians in typically viewing markets as institutions generating socially injurious levels of income and wealth inequality, have failed adequately to appreciate the social advances those same markets help to achieve. For markets have proven to be essential in the achieving of modern economic growth. Markets not only produce inequality; their use also can reduce poverty by facilitating development. Such an accomplishment should not be trivialized. With that development typically comes a rising level of educational attainment, an accomplishment necessary for a citizenry to be effectively self-governing.

Furthermore, the elimination of markets has been at the root of much of what went wrong with communism, from the forced collectivization of agriculture in the former Soviet Union in the 1920s to the Great Leap Forward in China in the 1950s. In the absence of markets guiding economic decisions, centralized allocation is required, all too often resulting in the use of coercion and force. Under those circumstances democracy has no chance.[7]

---

[5] Ibid., p. 129, 145.

[6] Ibid., p. 126.

[7] On this subject see Alex Nove, "Marx, the Market and 'feasible socialism'," in Alec Nove *Socialism, Economics and Development*, (London: Allen & Unwin 1985, pp. 51-62. Nove's views on the role of markets in socialism are contained in Alex Nove, *The Economics of Feasible Socialism* (London: George Allen & Unwin, 1983), especially pp. 1-67.

Dunn thus fails adequately to explore the extent to which the frontier of democracy can be advanced in the presence of a market economy. To be sure, he does write that "the big question" is "how much of the distant order of equality can still be rescued from the ruins of its overwhelming defeat." But his answer is vague, holding out only the hope that "the imagery of a democratic way of life bites very deep and summons up intense imaginative energies." What is most conspicuous in this regard is Dunn's failure to follow up his own insight into the role of wealth in the political system by exploring what could be done about it.[8] It is precisely because political equality is a strongly held value that it is possible that those "imaginative energies" of its advocates might find ways to prevent the economic inequality that markets create from distorting the political process.

Like Dunn, other theorists of democracy are aware of the problem of the political dominance of wealth. But what often occurs in the literature is that the problem is acknowledged but then not rigorously analyzed. Thus Ian Shapiro discusses the undemocratic consequences of the fact that "politicians must compete for campaign contributions in order to be in a position to compete for votes," but offers no sustained discussion on the subject.[9] Similarly, Robert A. Dahl writes that "because market capitalism inevitably creates [economic] inequalities, it limits the democratic potential ...by creating inequalities in the distribution of political resources." But Dahl has little to say about how to correct this problem. He says only that making the political system in market capitalism more democratic "is a profoundly difficult question for which there are no easy answers and certainly no brief ones."[10]

This abdication of responsibility by intellectuals has come at a considerable cost. It has meant that the range of policy options that could increase political equality is narrow. There are a multitude of publicists and authors

---

[8] John Dunn, *Setting the People Free*, p. 168, 172.
[9] Ian Shapiro, *The State of Democratic Theory* (Princeton and Oxford: Princeton University Press, 2003), p. 59.
[10] Robert A. Dahl, *On Democracy* (New Haven and London: Yale University Press, 1998) 177, 179.

subsidized by the wealthy who offer arguments about the virtues of markets and the risks associated with impeding the right of rich people to freely deploy their resources in the political realm.[11] These dominate the intellectual landscape not because of the strength of their arguments, but rather by default. Because there has been so little academic discussion of the economics of democratic processes, the development of a framework identifying a mechanism to achieve a more egalitarian political order has been stunted.

The counterpart to this neglect of theory has been the failure by liberal and radical political activists to champion the issue. Obviously if reducing the role of wealth in the political process were to be attractive to anyone it would be to the political left. But not even the Socialist Party during the period of its greatest strength in the United States, the years before World War I, worked to achieve that goal. Like similar socialist and communist parties elsewhere, it sought the chimera of public ownership of the economy as its long term goal and in the process neglected to argue that the electoral process should be treated as a public good. More immediately it engaged in struggles for concrete objectives such as union rights, minimum wage legislation and unemployment insurance, ignoring how politics is paid for.[12]

Similarly the coalition that provided the political foundation in the 1930s for the New Deal did not actively seek changes in political campaign funding. Perhaps most surprisingly, it was not even a part of the New Left's call for a participatory democracy in the early 1960s. The Port Huron Statement, written for and by the Students for a Democratic Society, makes no mention of the need to finance the electoral process in a way to achieve the students' goal of greater social and economic equality. The Statement discusses the civil rights movement, the peace movement, the need for a revitalized labor movement, and civil

---

[11] See for example, John Samples (ed.) *Welfare for Politicians? Taxpayer Financing of Campaigns* (Washington DC: Cato Institute, 2005) and Bradley A. Smith, *Unfree Speech: The Folly of Campaign Finance Reform* (Princeton and Oxford: Princeton University Press, 2001).

[12] James Weinstein, *The Long Detour: The History and Future of the American Left* (Cambridge MA: 2003), p. 47.

liberties, but there is no discussion at all about the how candidates for office should be funded.[13]

Rather than challenging the financing of the electoral system, the American left has typically focused on discrimination, championing equal rights for racial and ethnic minorities, women, and marginalized groups such as gays, lesbians, and transgendered people. It has also actively supported limitations on greenhouse gas emissions and has strongly opposed United States military interventions overseas. But with very few exceptions, neither socialists, liberals, nor progressives have prioritized promoting an alternative to the role of private wealth in elections. They have concentrated instead on the outcome of politics, rather than on the political process. Scandals such as Watergate and the unregulated use of "soft money" did force campaign finance reform onto the legislative agenda. But FECA's passage in 1974 and BCRA's in 2002 were both driven by revelations of corruption, not by a movement seeking to reconstruct the political system to achieve greater participant equality.

As was the case with academic theorists, it is not as if inequities present in the political system were unrecognized by activists. They well understood that the power of wealth placed their movements at a serious political disadvantage. But they simply assumed that, though wealth would line up against them, the advocates of reform would be able to generate an adequate countervailing power to secure victories. The indifference to campaign finance reform on the left reflected an implicit judgment that devoting energy and resources to that objective would result in fewer achievements than would working for specific political outcomes.

Left activism in American history has scored significant victories in breaking down barriers of prejudice and discrimination. These successes, as intellectual historian Paul Lyons notes, made "our society more inclusive, more fair, [and] more just...." In measuring such accomplishments, Lyons writes:

---

[13] "The Port Huron Statement," in Judith Clavir Albert and Stewart Edward Albert (eds.) *The Sixties Papers: Documents of a Rebellious Decade* (New York: Praeger, 1984), pp 176-196.

"keep in mind how deep racial prejudice runs; how profound it is historically to seek equality for women both in the workplace and with more difficulty, within the family; how powerful homophobia has been within our culture; how much of our civilization has rested on the notion that nature is available for conquest, domination. Now consider how much has changed over the past thirty to forty years in each instance."[14] The changes achieved, in short, were substantial.

So too though were the political costs. Left activism generated, as Lyons argues, resentment from "everyday people" who did not identify with or benefit from those changes. It would be "most unusual," Lyons writes, if individuals "mostly concerned with making a living and raising their families, could immediately or even in a short period of time integrate these fundamental challenges into their behaviors and their consciousness."[15] Segments of the population were lost to progressives because the latter did not posses an inclusive and unifying message, a set of proposals that would speak to, assuage, or compensate people who believed that they were required to shoulder the costs of change. What the left needed, but did not possess, was a politics that transcended specific constituencies and their concerns, that could speak to the aspirations of people beyond the groups whose interests it championed. In its absence too many people could reasonably see liberals as working on behalf of special interests with whom they did not identify.

Even as barriers to full participation in the life of society were breaking down, seemingly unnoticed was the fact that the political system itself was becoming more oligarchic. As we saw in Chapter 1, between 1974 and 2006 Congressional campaign expenditures increased by more than four-fold. All of this money was raised from private sources. While the society was becoming socially more liberal, the political process ironically became increasingly dependent upon and thereby shaped by a relatively small number of wealthy

---

[14] Paul Lyons, *American Conservatism: Thinking It, Teaching It* (Nashville: Vanderbilt University Press, 2009) p. 15.
[15] Ibid., p. 14, 15.

political donors. This reconfiguration went largely unchallenged by progressives. Thus at the same time that a substantial fraction of the American electorate came to resent the cultural turmoil that it associated with the left, the political process increasingly reflected the preferences of a resurgent political right, financed by wealthy individuals who stood to benefit from such a shift. In this way, two forces in combination provided fuel for the conservative ascendancy of recent decades. On one hand the identity politics that did so much to make American society more tolerant and fair alienated numerically important segments of the population. And at the same time the dominance of wealth in the political process strengthened the free market politics that rich people sought.

They were able to implement their conservative agenda because their call for a reduction in the size of the public sector resonated with a public that was becoming increasingly distrustful of the government. Polling data since that early 1970s have been clear in reporting that a substantial percentage of Americans believe that government policies are tools of special interests and will not effectively address their concerns.[16] With this the case the political right was at a distinct advantage compared to the left. The latter's typical call for expanded government programs was met with skepticism if not outright hostility. At least in part this opposition was rooted in the reality that only those policies approved of by wealthy donors could become law. With that the case, for many people government policies would result only in increased taxes with nothing to show for this loss of income.

But as we have seen by allowing the country's political agenda to remain responsive to and dominated by big campaign contributors, the problem of greenhouse gas emissions was evaded, the health care sector remained expensive and inefficient, and Wall Street succeeded in having its deregulation agenda implemented, resulting in a devastating economic crisis. In short, the political process became dysfunctional, failing the country and its people. It was unable to

[16] Jay R. Mandle, *Democracy, America and the Age of Globalization*, 99-107.

address important problems successfully and it itself contributed to the creation of others. If the left was not responsive to the concern that the government was not to be trusted, the right similarly had no answers to the mounting problems that confronted American society.

In the past, theorists of democracy have been concerned that popular rule might threaten a smoothly functioning economy. As Charles S. Maier writes, the history of democracy in the nineteenth and twentieth centuries "involves the story not so much of making the world safe for democracy...but of making democracy safe for the world." Dating back to Madison, de Tocqueville, and Schumpeter, the worry has been that democracy would produce a counterproductive politics of expropriation. The masses in political ascendancy might, it was feared, use their new-found power to massively redistribute wealth. Democracy might become, in Maier's words "a voracious mass confiscatory force," heedless of the economic damage it might inflict.[17]

The contemporary power of political wealth has created a situation which resembles the reverse of these concerns. Because politics has become more expensive and its financing narrowly based, the worry that wealth will not be adequately represented in the political process cannot be taken seriously. The reality is the opposite. Money in politics has become so important that the scope of popular rule has been narrowed. It is equality that today is in need of rescue.

Nevertheless, still today the belief persists among liberals that progressive objectives can be secured without a systemic change in political financing. The rapturous welcome accorded to Barack Obama's candidacy, despite the fact that his campaign was privately funded and largely dependent upon big donors in its critical early efforts, reflects this continued belief that the power of money can be overcome. In Obama's case the anticipation was that a progressive President

---

[17] Charles S. Maier, "Democracy Since the French Revolution," in John Dunn (ed.) *Democracy: The Unfinished Journey: 508 BC to AD 1993* (Oxford: Oxford University Press, 1992), p. 126, 127.

would be able to tame money. Ignored was the possibility that big money would succeed in taming the progressive President.

Whether Obama's term in office ends in four or eight years, his administration will be judged by the degree of its success in moving Congress to legislate promised changes: bringing the financial sector under meaningful regulation so as to spare the country future economic catastrophes; scaling back green house emissions to avoid the environmental calamities that the Intergovernmental Panel on Climate Change has forecast; and radically reforming the country's health care system in a way that extends health insurance coverage to those who otherwise would go uninsured and at the same time curtails the medical system's escalating costs.

Progressives have placed their bets on the charismatic president. But if that bet is lost and Obama's incumbency ends with these issues still unresolved, it is conceivable that the left will react by reconsidering its priorities. It might then judge that no matter how sincere a progressive a president might be, the power of money today is so great that even the level of popular support for change that Obama embodies will, with the current political funding system, always be ineffective. The likelihood of such an outcome increased in January 2010 when the Supreme Court handed down its precedent-shattering Citizens United v. Federal Election Commission decision. That decision overturned a ban on corporate political spending, thereby removing prohibitions on such expenditures dating from the 1907 Tillman Act.[18] Indeed, President Obama himself worried that with that ruling, as he put it, "the Supreme Court has given a green light to a new stampede of special interest money in our politics. It is a major victory for big oil, Wall Street banks, health insurance companies and the other powerful interests that marshal their power every day in Washington to drown out the

---

[18] Supreme Court of the United States, Citizens United v. Federal Election Commission, 558 __(2010), http://www.supremecourtus.gov/opinions/09pdf/08-205.pdf.

voices of everyday Americans."[19] With this the case, reforming the way politics is financed might – out of a sense of necessity – become a central part of the liberal agenda. In that sense the Obama presidency may represent a fundamental turning point in the politics of the political left, and perhaps even that of the country.

If this were to happen, the political left would be returning to a strategy similar to that adopted in the 1830s and 1840s with the rise of the Chartist Movement in Great Britain. Chartism was the first working class movement spawned by the industrial revolution. The most important element in its insurgency was the belief that the democratization of British politics was required if the deprivations of the era were to be corrected. Politics could meet the challenge of misery. But while democratization for the Chartists meant universal suffrage, today when the right to vote has largely been secured, democratization means something else: financing elections in a way that is consistent with their character as a public good. But the sensibility is the same. An egalitarian democracy is the vehicle for the solving of social problems.

Treating the electoral process as a public good is the necessary step that has to be taken to rebalance the relationship between the economy and politics. The latter should be a zone of equality, precisely because inequality prevails in the former. A wall between the two spheres is necessary in order to protect political egalitarianism. The public funding of political campaigns would go far to establish such a wall. It would provide for autonomy in the legislative process, freeing politicians from the thralldom associated with private campaign fundraising. In a "clean elections" setting, business people like all citizens, would be entitled to lobby and present their ideas in an attempt to persuade lawmakers of their points of view. But the power they possess as the paymasters of political careers would be lost. With that the case, their success in influencing policy would be dependent on the strength of their arguments, not on the amount of money they had contributed.

---

19 Adam Liptak, "Ruling on Spending May Alter Political Terrain," *The New York Times*, January 22, 2010, http://www.nytimes.com.

Lyons argues that if progressives are to be successful "they must find way to tap into the deep reservoirs of egalitarianism that once were the bread and butter of all left-of-center movements."[20] That unifying issue could have been – and might still be – political equality. If such a platform were advanced, it would be possible to argue that liberals - while still endorsing advances for environmentalists, gays, women and people of color – could appeal to the group Lyons calls "white mainstream people" as well.[21] It might under those circumstances be able to contest the right-wing backlash more successfully than in the past. A movement that seeks to reduce the role of wealth in politics in the name of equality may not be the only way to achieve this unifying objective. But it stands out as perhaps the most realistic and accomplishable way of staking out that claim.

The public ownership of the political process, as opposed to its current private ownership, can become the goal that could characterize a new and inclusive political left. It is true that a modern economy cannot efficiently function if it is centrally controlled. Markets and private initiatives are needed. But the reverse is true with regard to the political process. In the electoral process, private funding is inefficient: with it the interests of the whole society are poorly served. The argument would be that what the country needs is something very nearly the opposite of the old socialist paradigm. Instead of nationalizing the economy and placing a low priority on mechanisms of democratic rule, the economy should remain in private hands but be subject to rules established by a political sphere of equality.

---

[20] Ibid., p. 15.
[21] Ibid., p. 15.

Bibliography

ANES Guide to Public Opinion and Electoral Behavior, http://www.electionstudies.org/nesguide/totable/tab6b _5.htm

Albert, Judith Clavir and Stewart Edward Albert (eds.) *The Sixties Papers: Documents of a Rebellious Decade* (New York: Praeger, 1984

Alexander, Herbert E., *Financing the 1960 Election* (Princeton N.J.: Citizen's Research Foundation, n.d.)

American Environics, *Energy Attiitudes: An Analysis of Opinion Research on Energy and Global Warming*, (American Environics, 2007)

Ansolabehere, Stephen, John M. deFigueiredo and James M. Snyder Jr. "Why is There So Little Money in U.S. Politics," *The Journal of Economic Perspectives*, Vol. 17, no. 1 (Winter, 2003)

Bartels, Larry M., *Unequal Democracy: The Political Economy of the New Gilded Age* (Princeton and Oxford: Princeton University Press, 2008)

Bloomberg Poll on Obama, Health Care, Economy: Results Chart, September 16, 2009, http://www.bloomberg.com/

Blumenthal, David and James A. Morone, *The Heart of Power: Health and Politics in the Oval Office* (Berkeley, Los Angeles, London: University of California Press, 2009)

Breaking Free with Fair Elections: A New Declaration of Independence for Congress, (N.P: Brennan Center for Justice, Common Cause, Democracy Matters, Public Campaign, Public Citizen, and U.S. PIRG, March 2007)

Breakthrough Institute, "National Energy Education Act," www.thebreakthrough.org

Broder, John M., "House Passes Bill to Address Threat of Climate Change," *The New York Times*, June 27, 2009. http://nytimes.com

Bottomore, Tom, "Introduction," Joseph A. Schumpeter, *Capitalism, Socialism and Democracy*, (First edition, 1942; New York, HarperPerennial, 1976)

"Buckley et al. v. Valeo,, Secretary of the United States Senate et al, 424 U.S. 1, http://www.epic.org/free_speech/buckley_v_valeo.html
Campaign Finance Institute, *Presidential Candidates' Fundraising Activities*, for *Selected time periods,. http://www.cfinst.org*

Center for Responsive Politics, "A Brief History of Money in Politics: Campaign Finance and Campaign Finance Reform in the United States," *http://www.campaignfinancesite.org/history/reform1.html*

Center for Responsive Politics, "Totals by Sector," "Where the Money Came From," "Donor Demographics," "PACs by Industry," "Barack Obama: Industries," "House Financial Services Committee, 111th Congress (2008 cycle): Overview" and "Senate Banking, Housing and Urban Affairs Committee, 111th Congress (2008 cycle) http://www.opensecrets.org

Cmar, Thomas "Toward a Small Donor Democracy: The Past and Future of Incentive Programs for Small Political Contributions," *Fordham Urban Law Journal*, Vol 32, no. 443 (2005)

Corrado, Anthony "Money and Politics: A History of Federal Campaign Finance Law," in Anthony Corrado, Daniel R. Ortiz, Thomas E. Mann and Trevor Potter (eds.) *The New Campaign Finance Sourcebook* (Washington DC: The Brookings Institution, 2005)

Dahl, Robert A. *On Democracy* (New Haven and London: Yale University Press, 1998)

Demyank, Yuliya and Otto Van Hemert, "Understanding the Sub-Prime Mortgage Crisis," *http://wwrm/cp/abstract=1020396*

DeNavas-Walt, Carmen, Bernadette D. Proctor and Jessica C. Smith, U.S. Census Bureau, Current Population Reports, P60-236, Income , *Poverty and Health Insurance Coverage in the United States, 2008* (Washington DC: U.S. Government Printing Office, 2009)

Dunn, John "Conclusion," in John Dunn (ed.) *Democracy: The Unfinished Journey, 508 BC to AD 1993* (Oxford: Oxford University Press, 1992), p. 260

-------------*Setting the People Free: The Story of Democracy* (London: Atlantic Books, 2005)

Easterlin, Richard A. *Growth Triumphant: The Twenty-First Century in Historical Perspective* (Ann Arbor: The University of Michigan Press, 1996)

Energy Information Administration, *Monthly Energy Review*, June 2008

Financing Presidential Campaigns: Report of the President's Commission on Campaign Costs, Financing Presidential Campaigns (April 1962)

Fortune 500, "Top Industries: Most Profitable, Return on Shareholders' Equity." *http://money.cnn.com/magazines/fortune/fortune*500/2008

Francia, Peter L., John C. Green, Paul S. Herrnson, Lynda W. Powell, and Clyde Wilcox, *The Financiers of Congressional Elections: Investors, Ideologues and Intimates* (New York: Columbia University Press, 2003)

Goodman Peter S., "Taking Hard New Look at a Greenspan Legacy," *The New York Times*, October 9, 2008, *http://www.nytimes.com*

Gould, Lewis L., "The Progressive Era," in Lewis L. Gould (ed.) *The Progressive Era* (Syracuse: Syracuse University Press, 1974)

Graf, Joseph, Grant Reeher, Michael J. Malbin, Costas Panagopoulis. *Small Donors and Online Giving: A Study of Donors to the 2004 Presidential Campaigns,* Institute for Politics, Democracy and the Internet, http:www.ipdo.org

John C. Green, "Financing the 2004 Presidential Nomination Campaigns," in David B. Magleby, Anthony Corrado and Kelly D. Patterson (eds.) *Financing the 2004 Election* (Washington DC: Brookings Insitution Press, 2006)

John C. Green and Nathan S. Bigelow, "The 2000 Presidential Nominations: The Costs of Innovation," in David B. Magleby (ed.) *Financing the 2000 Election* (Washington DC: The Brookings Insitution, 2002)

Haines, Michael R., "Conditions of Work and the Decline of Mortality," in Roger Schofield and David Reher, "The Decline in Mortality in Europe," in R. Schofield, D. Reher and A. Bideau (eds.) *The Decline in Mortality in Europe* (Oxford: Clarendon Press, 1991)

Hamburger, Tom and Kim Geiger, "Health Insurers Get Upper Hand," *Los Angeles Times*, August 24, 2009
http://www/latimes.com/news/nationworld/washingtondc/la-na-healthcare-insurers24-2009aug24,0,4551786.story

Heard, Alexander, *The Costs of Democracy: Financing American Political Campaigns* (Garden City: Anchor Books, 1962; first published, 1960)

Hofstadter, Richard, *The Age of Reform: From Bryan to F.D.R.* (New York Vintage Books, 1955)

Hoogenboom, Ari, *Outlawing the Spoils: A History of the Civil Service Reform Movement, 1865-1883*, (Urbana: University of Illinois Press, 1961)

------------ "The Pendleton Act and the Civil Service," *The American Historical Review*, Vol. 64, no. 2 (January 1959)

Keyssar, Alexander, *The Right to Vote: The Contested History of Democracy in the United States* (New York: Basic Books, 2000)

Kuttner, Robert, *The Squandering of America: How the Failure of Our Politics Undermines Our Prosperity* (New York: Alfred A. Knopf, 2007)

Library of Congress, *The Federalist Papers, Federalist No. 10*, "The Same Subject Continued: The Union as a Safeguard Against Domestic Faction and Insurrecton," November 23, 1787,
http://thomas.loc.gov/home/histdox/fed_10.html.

Joe, Wesley Y., Michael J. Malbin, Clyde Wilcox, Peter W. Brusoe and Jamie P. Pimlott, *Do Small Donors Improve Representation? Some Answers from Recent Gubernatorial and State Legislative Elections*, (Washington DC: Campaign Finance Institute 2008)

Kaiser, The Henry J Family Foundation, *Kaiser Health Tracking Poll (July 7-14, 2009)*, Publication #7943, www.kff.org

Keyhani, Salomeh, and Alex Federman, "Doctors on Coverage – Physicians' Views on a New Public Insurance Option and Medicare Expansion, *The New England Journal of Medicine*, September 14, 2009, www.nejm.org

Kuznets, Simon, "Modern Economic Growth: Findings and Reflections," in Simon Kuznets, *Population, Capital and Growth* (New York: W.W. Norton & Company Inc., 1973)

Lyons, Paul, *American Conservatism: Thinking It, Teaching It* (Nashville: Vanderbilt University Press, 2009)

Maier, Charles S., "Democracy Since the French Revolution," in John Dunn (ed.) *Democracy: The Unfinished Journey: 508 BC to AD 1993* (Oxford: Oxford University Press, 1992)

Malbin, Michael J., *Small Donors, Large Donors and the Internet: The Case for Public Financing after Obama*, (Washington DC: The Campaign Finance Institute, April 2009)

------------------ "Rethinking the Campaign Finance Agenda," *The Forum*, Vol. 6, no 1 (2008), The Berkeley Electronic Press, Article 3

------------------ and Sean A. Cain, *The Ups and Downs of Small and Large Donors* (Washington DC: The Campaign Finance Institute, 2007 *www.CFInst.org*)

Mann, Thomas E. and Michael J. Malbin, *Vital Statistics on Congress, 2008* (Washington DC: Brookings Institution Press, 2008)

Malhotra, Neil, "The Impact of Public Financing on Electoral Competition: Evidence from Arizona and Maine," *State Politics and Policy Quarterly*, Vol. 8, No. 3 (Fall 2008)

Mandle, Jay R., *Democracy, America and the Age of Globalization* (New York: Cambridge University Press, 2008)

McGerr, Michael, *A Fierce Discontent: The Rise and Fall of the Progressive Movement in America, 1870-1920* (New York: Free Press, 2003)

McGovern, George S., "It's Simple: Medicare for All," *The Washington Post*, September 13, 2009, http://www.washingtonpost.com

Mellor, Chip, "Three Lessons from Arizona," in John Samples (ed.) *Welfare for Politicians: Taxpayer Financing of Campaigns* (Washington DC: Cato Institute, 2005)

Miller, Michael G., "Public Money, Candidate Time and Electoral Outcomes in State Legislative Elections,"
http://www.nyaapor.org/pdfs/2008StudentPaperWinnerMiller.pdf?cff7f010

Morris, Charles R., The Two Trillion Dollar Meltdown: Easy Money, High Rollers and the Great Credit Crash (New York: Public Affairs, 2008; Kindle Edition)

Mutch, Robert E., "The First Federal Campaign Finance Bills," in Paul Baker (ed.), *Money and Politics* (University Park, PA, (The Pennsylvania State University Press, 2002)

-------------, *Campaigns, Congress and Courts: The Making of Federal Campaign Finance Law* (New York: Praeger, 1988)

Nelson, Michael, "A Short, Ironic History of American National Bureaucracy," *The Journal of Politics*, Vol. 44, no. 3

Nordhaus, Ted and Michael Shellenberger, *Break Through: From the Death of Environmentalism to the Politics of Possibility* (Boston and New York: Houghton Mifflin Company, 2007)

Nove, Alex, "Marx, the Market and 'feasible socialism'," in Alec Nove *Socialism, Economics and Development*, (London: Allen & Unwin 1985)

------------, *The Economics of Feasible Socialism* (London: George Allen & Unwin, 1983)

Ornstein, Norman J., Thomas E. Mann and Michael J. Malbin, *Vital Statistics on Congress 2008*, Washington D.C: Brookings Institution Press, 2008)

Overacker, Louise, *Money in Elections* (Reprint Edition New York: Arno Press, 1974); first published by The Macmillan Company, 1932

Patterson Kelly D., "Spending in the 2004 Election," in David B. Magleby, Anthony Corrado and Kelly D. Patterson (eds.) *Financing the 2004 Election* (Washington DC: The Brookings Institution, 2006)

Rehm, Diane, Transcript of The Diane Rehm Show, "Public Financing for the Presidential Campaign," Tuesday April 15, 2008 (Transcripts by Soft Scribe LLC).

Reich, Robert, "How Pharma and Insurance intend to Kill the Public Option, And What Obama and the Rest of Us Must Do, *Wall Street Pit*, June 6, 2009, http://www.wallstreetpit.com

Reid T. R., *The Healing of America: A Global Quest for Better, Cheaper and Fairer Health Care* (New York: The Penguin Press, 2009)

Reuters, "Factbox: Details of Baucus Plan for U.S. Healthcare Reform," September 17, 2009, *http://www.reuters.com/articlePrinct?articleID=US* TRE58G3250090917

Roques, Fabien A., William J. Nutall, David M. Newbery and Richard de Neufville, "Nuclear Power: A Hedge Against Uncertain Gas and Carbon Prices," *The Energy Journal*, Vol. 27, no. 4

Rorabaugh, W.J., *The Real Making of the President: Kennedy, Nixon and the 1960 Election (*Lawrence KS: University Press of Kansas, 2009)

Shapiro Ian, *The State of Democratic Theory* (Princeton and Oxford:, Princeton University Press, 2003)

Schmitt, Mark, "Mismatching Funds: How Small-Donor Democracy Can Save Campaign Finance Reform," *Democracy: A Journal of Ideas*, Issue #4 (Spring 2007) *http://www.democracyjournal.org/article.php?ID=6516*

Schumpeter, Joseph A., *Capitalism, Socialism and Democracy*, (First edition, 1942; New York, HarperPerennial, 1976)

Seelye, Katharine Q., "Medicare for All? 'Crazy,' 'Socialized' and Unlikely," *The New York Times*, September 19, 2009, http://prescriptions.blogs.nytimes.com

Simms, R.E.H. et al, "Energy Supply" in *Climate Change 2007 – Mitigation of Climate Change, Working Group III Contribution the Fourth Assessment Report of the Intergovernmental Panel on Climate Change 2007*, (New York: Cambridge University Press, 2007

Smith, Bradley A., *Unfree Speech: The Folly of Campaign Finance Reform* (Princeton and Oxford: Princeton University Press, 2001)

Sorauf, Frank J., *Money in American Elections* (Glenview: Scott, Foresman and Company, 1988)

Stiglitz, Joseph A., "Capitalist Fools," *Vanity Fair*, January 2009, *http://www.vanityfair.com/magazine/2009/01/stigltiz200901*

Summers, Mark Wahlgren, "'To Make the Wheels Revolve We Must Have Grease' Pork Barrel Politics in the Gilded Age," in Paula Baker (ed.) *Money and Politics*, (University Park PA: The Pennsylvania State University Press, 2002)

Sunstein Cass R., "The Enlarged Republic – Then and Now," *The New York Review of Books*, March 26, 2009

Supreme Court of the United States, McConnell v. Federal Election Commission 540 U.S _(2003), 118, http://www.law.cornell.edu/pdf/02-1674P.zo

Sutch, Richard and Susan B. Carter (eds.) *Historical Statistics of the United States, Earliest Times to the Present* (New York: Cambridge University Press, 2006)

Terhune, Chad and Keith Epstein, "The Health Insurers Have Already Won," *BusinessWeek*, August 6, 2009. *http://www.businessweek.com/print/magazine/content/09_33/b4143034820260.htm*

Thayer, George, *Who Shakes the Money Tree? American Campaign Financing Practices from 1789 to the Present* (New York: Simon and Schuster, 1973)

Trippi, Joe, *The Revolution Will Not Be Televised: Democracy, the Internet and the Overthrow of Everything* (New York: Regan Books, 2004)

Twentieth Century Fund/Century Foundation Working Group on Campaign Finance Litigation, *Buckley Stops Here*, Drafted by E. Joshua Rozenkranz (New York: The Century Foundation Press, 1998)

U.S. Census Bureau, *Statistical Abstract of the United States: 2009* (Washington D.C. 2008)

-------------- "Evidence from Census 2000 about Earnings by Detailed Occupation for Men and Women," (Issued May 2004), Figure 3. http://www.census.gov/prod/2004pubs/censr-15.pdf

U.S. Congressional Budget Office, Douglas W. Elmendorf, Director, "Letter to Honorable Charles B. Rangel, Chairman, Committee on Ways and Means, U.S. House of Representatives, July 17, 2009

United States General Accounting Office, *Financial Derivatives: Actions Needed to Protect the Financial System* (Washington D.C.: General Accounting Office, May 1994

--------------- *Advanced Energy Technologies: Budget Trends and Challenges for DOE's Energy R&D Program*, March 5, 2008, *http://www/gao.gov/new.items/d08556t.pdf*

"United States House Prices," http://mysite.verizon.net/vzeqrguz/housingbubble

Walsh, Bryan, "Clean Energy: U.S. Lags in Research and Development," *Time*, August 1, 2009, *http://www.time.com*

Weinstein, James, *The Long Detour: The History and Future of the American Left* (Cambridge MA: 2003)

White House, The, Office of the Press Secretary, "Remarks by the President at the National Academy of Sciences Annual Meeting," April 27, 2009. http://www.whitehouse.gov.

--------------- "Remarks by the President to a Joint Session of Congress on Health Care," http://www.whitehouse.gov

--------------- "The Obama Plan: Stability and Security for all Americans," *http://www.whitehouse.gov/issues/health_care/plan*

Wiley, Joe, Michael Malbin, Clyde Wilcox Pete Brusoe and Jamie Pimlett, *Do Small Donors Improve Representation?* (Campaign Finance Institute, 2008) http://www.cfinst.org

Zeleny, Jeff and and Michael Luo, "Public Financing? Obama and McCain Appear Split," *The New York Times*, April 10, 2008, *http://www.nytimes.com*

Zelizer Julian E., "Seeds of Cynicism: The Struggle over Campaign Finance, 1956-1974," in Paula Baker (ed.) *Money and Politics* (University Park PA" The Pennsylvania State University Press, 2002)

Index